D0862403

Get Your Foot
Out of the
Durn Petunias

Get Your Foot Out of the Durn Petunias

Stories From My Life

Marj Carpenter

To order additional copies of this book, contact:
Xlibris Corporation
1-888-795-4274
www.Xlibris.com
Orders@Xlibris.com
74465

Dedication

These unusual stories from my life are dedicated to my three children; Carolyn, Jim Bob and Cathy who lived through a lot of them with me. I could never have made it without them.

A *Country Gal*

Marj Carpenter was just a country gal born in Mercedes, Texas, with very few plans for the future, other than wanting to be a reporter.

But, her life mushroomed into covering interesting murders, scandals, and politics. Then, it mushroomed again into covering Presbyterian mission work in 126 countries.

She went on to become president of the National Federation of Press Women in 1992. In 1995 she became Moderator of the 207th General Assembly of the Presbyterian Church (U.S.A.)

It's difficult to tell her life story. It's easier to simply tell stories from her life.

Here they are . . .

First Section

Contents

Get Your Foot Out of the Durn Petunias 11

My First Murder Report 13

About Some Other Murders 16

And Wrecks and More Wrecks 19

I Was an Early Sports Reporter 22

And The Dangers of Sports Writing 25

A Little More About My Migrant Kids 30

And the Billie Sol Days 33

And There Were Bad Days 37

The Camera and I 41

Get Your Foot Out of the Durn Petunias

This book is full of stories about the life of Marj Carpenter. It is not a full autobiography because all of my life is not interesting. But it is stories from my life to help you understand how I got from there to here.

The story that gave this book its title will be my first one. It was 1964. It was the year after the Kennedy assassination. It was two years after the Billie Sol Estes scandal.

I was on vacation with my three children. One of the places I stopped was Washington, D.C. I had a very good friend there, a well-known reporter named Sarah McClendon.

You have probably seen her on television at Presidential press conferences. She was the little old lady in the back of the room who jumped up and said, "Mr. President, Mr. President." And usually upset him.

She had gotten permission for me to attend a press conference in which President Lyndon Johnson was going to sign an "across-the-board" pay raise for federal employees. She said she would take my children somewhere while I went to the press conference.

She asked the children, Cathy, 14, Carolyn, 12, and Jim Bob, 8, whom they would like to meet in Washington.

Before the girls could answer, Jim Bob popped up and said, "Smokey the Bear." Sarah informed him that Smokey the Bear was undoubtedly in New Mexico, not Washington, D.C. Jim Bob informed her that his funny book said that Smokey was in the Washington, D.C. zoo.

So they went to the Washington, D.C. zoo, and there he was. Sarah wrote a nationwide column about that. She said that in all her years in the capital city, that was a first. "Most people want to meet the President or a Supreme Court judge, a senator, a Congressman, or a cabinet member—not Smokey the Bear. But we had a good day. We also saw a white albino tiger."

In the meantime, I was getting final clearance to go into the press conference. Officials checked my credentials. They checked my camera. They then said, "Go straight ahead."

I did. I went straight ahead, pushed open a door, and went out onto a porch. Everybody jumped back, making room for me. I was in the wrong place. The porch group was expecting President Johnson.

Congressman-at-large, Joe Pool, from Texas, unhappily recognized me and said, "Marj Carpenter, what are you doing out here?" I explained. He then said, "Go back through the door, turn left, go down the hall, and out into the Rose Garden." I hastily retreated. I was sorry to embarrass him. When I got out into the garden, there were a lot of reporters, but no roses. I finally asked, "Where are the roses?" One of the other reporters looked at me in disdain and said, "Jackie Kennedy had them dug up. She put in seasonal flowers for each state, which change from month to month. This month is Kansas sunflowers and petunias."

"Oh," I said brilliantly, and thought to myself, "What a shame." I like roses.

Then suddenly, Lyndon came out on the porch. All of the members of the press surged forward at once, knocking everybody aside, trying to get a good position. I, too, surged, and my foot slipped over into the petunia bed. At this point, a secret service person grabbed my arm and said, "Lady, get your foot out of the durn petunias."

I did. But, as this book will tell you, my foot has been in the durn petunias most of my life.

My First Murder Report

I really think I was meant to be a reporter from the time I was born. I was born, incidentally, in Mercedes, a small Texas town on the border of Mexico. I was one of three children. My sister, Beatrice, had been killed in an accident with a horse shortly before I was born. My brother, Walter, who was two years older than me, was my hero.

But one day I remember being very angry at this hero. On Saturday, Mother used to assign Walter and me chores. One of us shook out all the throw rugs and rag rugs. One of us dusted the baseboards. We didn't like either job, and we alternated them from one Saturday to the next.

In return for doing the chores, we were given 25 cents. One nickel was immediately put aside for Sunday School. One nickel was immediately put aside for church. One nickel was dropped into an earthen container to save for Christmas money. That left two nickels.

Each Saturday afternoon, we walked a mile to town—Walter, Edward Covington, who lived across the field, and I. We each took our nickel, and we went to a cowboy show, wonderful movies with Tom Mix, Hopalong Cassidy, or Buck Jones.

With the other nickel, we could buy a hamburger or candy or a toy at Hanshaw's Dime Store. It was all rather wonderful and made Saturdays very special, after the baseboards were dusted and the rugs were shaken out.

But this particular Saturday, when I was four years old, was not special when it began. Little Harvey, my first cousin from down the Valley, had arrived with Aunt Elsie just as we were about to depart for the picture show.

We wanted him to get a nickel and come along, but Aunt Elsie said that cowboy movies were too violent for Little Harvey. Mother announced that since I was nearest Little Harvey's age, he was my guest, and I would stay and play with him while Walter and Edward went on to the show. You talk about a rotten deal. I was not happy, and Walter was no longer my hero.

After they left, I went and collected Walter's small car collection which he kept meticulously clean. We took them down into the muddy field between our house and my Grandpa Diehl's home.

Little Harvey and I sat down in the tall weeds and began to play with the cars. I was trying to get them as muddy as possible. Suddenly, we were startled when a man ran right past us, almost stepping on us. He kept running. We stood up in the tall weeds to see what was happening. To our amazement, a car jumped the curb and began to drive through our field in pursuit of the man on foot. There was another man standing on the running board of that car. I knew him. He went to our Presbyterian church. His name was Mr. Joust. He had a gun, and he shot the man who was running. The man on foot fell, and Little Harvey and I raced to stand over him when he said a few words in Spanish and became silent.

Suddenly, Mr. Joust was screaming. "Those are the Collier children. Get them out of here." He was half right. I was a Collier child. Harvey was a Diehl. Not only that, he was a Diehl that we were supposed to be keeping away from violence.

About then, my Grandpa arrived, all out of breath. He grabbed both Harvey and me from the back of our collars and ran off, carrying us up to his yard. He shouted, "Stay here! Don't move!" and he ran back to the scene.

Suddenly, more law cars arrived with flashing lights and screaming sirens. There was a lot of excitement. Part of the excitement was caused by Aunt Elsie, who was screaming from my Mother's back porch. I remember all of it.

Back in the beginning of the afternoon when Walter and Edward left for the show, they taunted me with, "Yaa-yaa-yaa. We're going to the show."

Well, I got even. As they came out of the picture show, they saw the police cars and ran all the way home, and Grandpa nailed them as they hit the edge of the yard and told them to stay there. At which point, I said, "Yaa-yaa-yaa. We saw the dead man." They were crestfallen, and I was full of myself.

At supper that night, I was still full of myself, as I reported my first murder scene. Little Harvey had long since been taken back home to McAllen. Dad told my Mother, "The man was full of marijuana and was shooting up the North Side. They shot him because they thought if he got across the road to the tall cornfield, they would lose him."

"I know, I know," piped up this new reporter. "Mr. Joust pulled out his gun and shot him dead."

Silence followed. It seems that Mr. Joust was a former Border Patrolman, retired, and no longer licensed to carry a gun. My Father said, "Marjorie, you are mistaken. Mr. Joust did not shoot that man."

"Daddy," I said, "I know him at church, and I was there. He did shoot that man, and the man died."

"Marjorie," says my Father, "You are never again to say Mr. Joust shot that man. I would not want to have to spank you." He frightened me so badly that even now, I use a false name for the shooter. I didn't want a spanking either. So I hushed and learned that day that you can't always report the news exactly like it happens. And I wanted to—oh, how I wanted to tell my story!

So, maybe I was just born to be a reporter.

About Some Other Murders

In my newspaper career, I covered a lot of murder scenes. That's sad, but true. I've been to the site where people were killed; I've been to the trials. I just can't begin to tell you about all of them. But it made me very sympathetic towards victims and with little sympathy for the culprits.

The worst murders are those committed by family members. I remember one in Andrews, Texas. They hadn't had a murder reported in eight years. It was a good, clean place to live.

One day I was in the residential area at a beauty shop in a home, getting a haircut. I heard sirens and a lot of commotion. I covered police news for that semi-weekly newspaper, so I went to the phone and called the sheriff's dispatcher, Delores.

Delores said, "Where are you?" And I told her. "Well," she said, "You're just two doors from the murder scene."

At which point, I ran out of the beauty shop and ran two doors down with my camera, which I had retrieved out of the car. The murder scene was awful. A diminutive, 5'2" woman was dead in the bathroom and had apparently been beaten to death with a hammer. The quite large, over six foot tall, husband was being hauled off in the sheriff's car. He had a minor scratch on his neck and was telling that his wife had tried to cut his throat.

I went around snapping pictures. One picture that I took was of a bloody telephone with bloody fingerprints all over it.

It seems, we later learned, that it was the first day to file income tax, and they had an argument about it at lunch. She had supposedly said she

16

was getting a divorce and would only file her own. One of the things that the husband alleged was that they had called their auditor and made an appointment. It was then, he said, that she turned on him.

Well, the telephone call became rather important evidence. The telephone that I had photographed was very important because it was obvious that somebody had made a call after they were already bloody. The lawmen checked the phone records, and there had only been one call. So I was called to court to testify about the bloody telephone.

On the day of the trial, I was sitting in a room where they hole up witnesses and didn't know that they had already asked the sheriff about the phone. When they put me on the stand, they asked about the telephone again, and they asked me about the picture which was entered as evidence. When they asked me what color the telephone was, I said, "Light blue." And everyone roared with laughter. I didn't know why. I found out later that when they asked the sheriff what color the telephone was, he said,

"Black, no, white, no, pink; I can't remember." But it was light blue. Reporters develop a habit of noticing things like that.

I moved from Andrews shortly after that trial; some of the friends or relatives of the man charged with murder called me and said I had better give them the pictures and the negatives of that telephone. I simply answered, "I don't have them. They belong to the newspaper." And that was the end of that threat. I think they were attempting to call for an appeal.

Another murder that I remember occurred outside of Pecos, Texas. A hitchhiker was found murdered and stuffed into a culvert beside the highway. In his hand was clutched a credit card—not his. The law, of course, traced the credit card to one Oscar Kernohan who had lived and worked in San Antonio and was in California. They arrested him and brought him back to Pecos.

While questioning him, the lawmen asked why he killed the hitchhiker. Without hesitation, he said, "Because he noticed the blood on the seat." "What blood was that?" the lawman asked, "The blood from when I killed my wife and child," he answered calmly. "Oh, come on," said the deputy. "Well, I did," he said. "They kept fussing and whining and complaining about the trip, and I pulled off the road, killed them, and buried them."

"Oh, sure," said the lawman, "Near here?" "As a matter of fact, yes," said Kernohan. The long and the short of it was that an entourage of us, including reporters and cameras, went to the burial site about 12 miles out of town, and sure enough, the bodies were there.

Then, there was Henry Marshall. I worked on The Pecos Independent, which did the expose' on Billie Sol Estes back in 1962. One of the figures involved in that whole investigation was Henry Marshall from Franklin, near College Station, Texas. He had worked for the office of the United States Department of Agriculture that allotted eminent domain cotton acreage to different people. This was acreage obtained from lake or road right-of-ways and other locations. It was very valuable acquisitions.

When the USDA began to question a lot of the cotton allotment transfers around Pecos, which were involved with Estes and some of his friends, a lot of the testimony would come to a point in the hearings where farmers would say, "Henry Marshall told us it was all right."

Well, long before the hearings ended, Marshall was found dead on his farm, and it was ruled a suicide. Very unlikely, since he had been shot twice in the back with a single shot, reloading rifle, and knocked in the back of the head; then, he apparently placed himself in a pickup and put a hose from the tailpipe inside the cab, and asphyxiated himself. Some twenty years later the case was reopened, and the Texas Rangers decided it was a murder. Surprise, surprise.

Well, that will give you a little taste of some of the murders that I covered as the Lord got me ready to work and write for the national office of the Presbyterian Church.

And Wrecks and More Wrecks

One of the news beats that I covered on small West Texas newspapers was wrecks. I took pictures of them, and I wrote about them. Actually, we started out at one newspaper taking turns to cover the wrecks because they often occur in the middle of the night. So we would each cover a week at a time.

But as the staff grew smaller, I seemed to end up with all of the wrecks. Pecos, Texas, was on the meat-grinding highway where a lot of wrecks occurred. People went to sleep on that long stretch.

I cannot begin to tell you how many hundreds of wrecks I went to during my career. The impact of them lodged so strongly in my brain that to this day, whenever I pass a wreck, I find myself looking at the position of the cars and determining who hit whom.

But I don't stop because I well remember when I started out covering wrecks, a patrolman once came over and chewed me out for my morbid curiosity in taking pictures of a wreck. I tiredly handed him my press pass, and he stomped away, but said no more.

I also remember that in Pecos when we had two rival newspapers, the reporter from the other paper once jumped into the patrol car, sat down, and was taking notes while the patrolman was talking on his radio to headquarters. When the patrolman finished talking, he got out, walked around the car, snatched the reporter out of the patrol car, and threw him against the railroad tracks. I was glad I hadn't gotten into the patrol car.

You'll be glad to know that I am not going to try to tell you about all of those hundreds of wrecks—but just a few so you understand the impact on my life. My late husband used to scream out when I got up during the night to answer the phone and then take off for a wreck. But since he was the one that had insisted that I go back to work, I didn't pay a whole lot of attention to his concern.

I remember one terrible wreck where fourteen were killed. I remember one where a speeding driver hit a little girl just stepping off a school bus, and I remember one on Salt Draw bridge. That bridge was too narrow, and it was on a major highway. It was then US80 and later Interstate Highway 20. Two trucks crashed on that bridge. One driver escaped without serious injury, and the other truck went into the ditch and caught afire. When I arrived, you could hear the driver screaming in the fire.

This had an impact on me, and I wrote a strong editorial about that bridge. The highway department came along, split the highway there, and built another bridge going one way. Then, they sent me a safety plaque for writing the article, but I can still hear that man screaming.

I remember one wreck in a dust storm where thirty cars piled up and somebody had to work their way from car to car, looking for a doctor. I remember one windy wreck when I ran out of film and knelt down by the side of the road to reload my camera. I heard one car stop, and a lady asked the patrolman, "Why don't you help that poor lady down on the ground over there?" The patrolman answered, "That poor lady down on the ground has covered more wrecks than I have, and she's putting film in that camera."

I remember a whiskey transport catching afire after an accident, and every time a new bottle would burst, the fire would change colors. It was green and purple and orange and was probably the prettiest wreck I ever saw.

In those days when we weren't so anxious to sue anybody that helped us, I remember when a patrolman put an injured driver into the back seat of my car and asked me to drive him the 25 miles to the hospital, rather than wait for an ambulance. When I pulled up in the emergency drive, a tough old nurse said, "Marj, get out of the driveway. We're waiting for an emergency." I answered back, "The emergency is in the back seat of my car."

I recall covering the beginning of a trash collectors' union meeting in Big Spring, Texas, at which I was not welcome. The following day, while I was covering police news, a pickup driven by the father of one of the organizers, suddenly started and headed straight for me when I was crossing the street. He hit me and knocked me over 20 feet into the air.

In that accident, I injured my back and broke my wrist, but I didn't die. One of the vertebrae in my back grew back around another one, and that is the reason I often wobble when I walk. That is not one of my favorite memories.

The only funny thing that I can remember about that incident is that when my son arrived at the hospital, I asked him to go pick up my car, which was parked at City Hall. He asked, "How badly is it damaged?" He didn't have a lot of faith in my driving. I answered, "Oh, the car's not hurt. I was on foot." Then, he did get angry, but I assured him that going after the driver was not going to help the situation one iota. He tried to reach his sisters for them to come and help; however, one of them was en route home from England for Christmas, and the other was laid up with the mumps. Such is life.

Dale Walton, one of the editors of the San Angelo Standard Times, drove over to Pecos one day and took me along with him out to the Department of Public Safety's powerful communication tower. It was located several miles outside of town. They made an arrangement so that I could telephone them every night at 10 P.M. and find out if there had been any fatal wrecks in all of West Texas—a large area. That newspaper, from that time on for many years, always had the information on fatal wrecks first.

The deal was struck. My children tell me, even today, that the last thing they heard at night as they were drifting off to sleep was me calling on the telephone: "653-4571—collect, please." I wonder if that's still the number for the San Angelo Standard times.

Let me tell one funny wreck story to end this catastrophe chapter. San Angelo called me late one night and asked me to go out to Orla and get a picture. "Somebody just hit the train." "Oh, come on," I said, "The train only goes through Orla once a week."

I didn't want to drive fifty miles each way for nothing, so I called Mrs. Cooksey, who lived near the tracks. "I'm afraid they're right," she said, "There's all kinds of lights and commotion over there." So, I went to Orla.

I Was an Early Sports Reporter

That was never in my plans, but most of my life has not been in my plans. I was working for The Pecos Independent in that small West Texas town. The sports writer had been sent to the basketball game in Carlsbad, New Mexico. On the way, he got tipsy and wrecked the company car.

The next game came along, and Oscar Griffin, the editor, looked at me and said, "Do you know anything about basketball?" "A little bit," I admitted. "I used to watch it in high school." "That's good enough," he said. "Take the camera, and cover the high school basketball game up at the gym." Well, I made the mistake of doing all right, and so I covered basketball. After basketball season, they asked if I knew baseball, and I said, "Oh, yes, I used to play baseball." So, I covered baseball . . . and then, track, golf, tennis, football, and eventually, even horse racing. I never did cover hockey or polo.

In West Texas, high school football games were often over a 100 miles away, and it meant a lot of driving. By the time I took on being a sports writer, my two girls were traveling with the Pecos band. So, my son, Jim Bob, and I went together to the games. I'd go to the press box, and he was on his own. Usually, he could find a buddy, but on one occasion, he got mud slung on him, simply because he was from Pecos.

When he later attended school in the rival town of Andrews, it got even more interesting. West Texans took their sports seriously. I remember one occasion in Pecos after Andrews won a basketball game, a group of students turned the bus over on its side with the Andrews team inside.

I remember once in Monahans after a fight the night before in Pecos at the victory bonfire, we got in a real row on the field after the game. The Monahans fire department came out and sprayed all of us with water.

I became quite a well-known sports writer and was always vocal. One time in Seminole after a baseball game, they threatened to put me in jail because I was so vocal about some of the calls. Seminole was always a bone of contention. You could not win a basketball game in the Seminole gymnasium. It was a combination of the enthusiasm of the fans there and how they were determined to protect that tradition. There was also the fact that they got to select the home officials.

One night I became famous among the other sports writers when I was sitting in the press box in that old gym, and the pigeons kept diving at us. Finally, I said, "Well, here we are in Seminole, and in this gym, you get the s—s one way or the other."

Another famous quote among the coaches was the story that I told them about the time that I taught migrant workers at Shelton Elementary in Odem, Texas. Those kids had a hard life. They had to pick cotton in late summer and early fall by hand. It was before the cotton stripper mechanical days. Then, they enrolled in school, at least in time for Christmas.

In the spring, they chopped weeds in cotton fields and sometimes went to Colorado "to cut the beets" for the sugar beet harvest. They were wonderful children, and I loved them dearly. There were almost fifty of them who were high school age and still in the grades; so, I asked to have an opportunity room. It was run like an old country school, and they could advance to high school, if they worked diligently.

In order to keep them interested, I used sports and music. I had a baseball team, and they were good. The pitcher was Faustino Lopez, and nobody could hit his pitches.

We played high school teams in practice games and usually won. They finally let us enter a high school tournament. We had no uniforms. The kids played in blue jeans, tee shirts, and worn-out tennis shoes. We had managed to get gloves, balls, and bats, and we had one catcher's mask.

I only had three substitute players. When the game was half over, those three replaced whichever three had not yet made a run. I didn't know much Spanish, but I could yell, "Correle!", which meant, "Run it!", and "Titole!", which meant, "Hit it!" We beat everybody. We won the high school tournament, and the coach from Mathis came up to me and said, "I don't mind so much being beaten by a woman coach, but being beaten by a pregnant woman coach who majored in music, is the last straw."

My daughter, Cathy, was born the following September.

And The Dangers of Sports Writing

Covering sports sometimes was very exciting and rewarding; although sometimes, it was downright dangerous.

I took pictures of sporting events in the years long before the telescopic lens was invented and put out for sale. So, I often had to stand very close to the game to get good photographs.

Of course, I worked for newspapers when they were still setting hot lead type on linotypes. If they got the big, old-fashioned press loaded, and the web broke, it took two or three hours to get all the little pieces of paper out of the press so you could start over.

One of the really funny things about hot lead was that when you lacked a name or information in your story, you had to make up something of the same length to save a spot where you could later insert it without resetting the entire story.

That got me in trouble one time. It was when they were still trying to make a women's editor out of me. They hadn't had much luck. They tried a cooking column, and I left the pumpkin out of the pumpkin cake; I got taken off that beat.

However, I was still writing weddings, and in Pecos, Texas, in those years, some weddings were really long and listed every little detail. The more prominent the bride, the longer the wedding write-up. Well, one of the bride's mothers forgot the name of an usher. I said we would just leave it out, but she had a fit. So, I put in a fake name, and she was to get me the real name later. I put in : John Q. Porkchop of Pocatello, Idaho.

She forgot to get me the real name. I forgot to take John Q. out of the story, and so she had a very unusual usher. She also had another fit.

Over in nearby Kermit one Saturday night, they used that same practice. They were electing Miss Kermit, a beauty queen. They left a spot on the front page for the picture and wrote the cutline, putting in Miss Prunella Prunewhip Was Named Miss Kermit Tonight. They put the picture in but forgot to take out Miss Prunella. I'm sure somebody had a fit over in Kermit. I sent a postcard to the newspaper and said that John Q. Porkchop would like to propose to Miss Prunella Prunewhip.

But back to sports . . . One time in Andrews, I was standing in close by third base, getting pictures, and a line drive, foul ball knocked me off my feet. It hit my right knee; that poor, right knee has taken a beating through the years.

One time when I was working for the church and had been traveling all day long, trying to get from Valentine, Nebraska, to Louisville, Kentucky, having gone without food and not much sleep, I fell down the escalator at the airport in Louisville and landed on that knee again.

Then, I landed on it in Albuquerque, New Mexico, when I checked into the hotel at the end of my moderator year, ran outside to try to get to another meeting, and it was raining. I hit wet pavement, slid and hit that knee again, as well as my head. I finally fell in my living room in 1998 and shattered my right thighbone. I think that entire leg had been weakened by then. In the year 2000, I was getting in a friend's car to go to dinner when her foot slipped off the brake, and the car rolled forward. There went my right hip.

You'd have thought an indoor basketball game would be safe, but once I was standing close to the line, and one of the cagers ran over me, knocking me into the wall. Needless to say, my picture was out of focus.

I guess the most hilarious incident was at a football game. I was running down the sideline, trying to get a shot of the player who was also running down the sideline. I hit the telephone wire of the coach's phone which led up to the press box phone. It was about ankle high. I fell splat into the mud. The entire crowd in the bleachers right behind me stood up and cheered. The player looked confused because he had been tackled before he got to the goal and couldn't understand why the home crowd was cheering.

At one point, it became dangerous for me to go to Seminole, Texas. They had avid sports fans there, and they hated nearby Andrews worse than anybody else. Their home team in Seminole was the Indians, and I had run a story in the Andrews County News about the girls' volleyball team winning and had called them Squaws. I got a very angry letter, telling me that their team name was the Royal Indian Maidens, not Squaws. Well, I wrote an apology—sort of. I apologized to the female athletes in Seminole, pointing out that the girls had won volleyball, track, and tennis. I said, "However, with the record, the Seminole boys have this year, they are the ones who should be called Squaws." As I look back on it, it is a wonder I wasn't pelted with rocks.

They wrote a right tacky column about me in the Seminole paper, which came out on the night Andrews fans were to be in town. I was with Nell Foster and Mona Tinsley, both of whom worked at Andrews High School. We stopped at all the newspaper machines, and I'd put in a quarter and take out all the papers. We filled that car with Seminole newspapers, and Mona would simply shut her eyes and say, "Ohhhhhh, no."

One time in Monahans, an angry basketball mother spit in my face. She literally leaned over the railing and spit very accurately. I recalled that incident later when I was in Albuquerque. By then, I had become a church reporter and then moderator of the Presbyterian Church. That year the gay lesbian group was demonstrating, and one of them spat in the face of the wife of a religion writer of whom they did not approve. I objected about this to one of the better-known lesbians and leader of the group. She told me, "Well, it has happened to us, too. You just don't know how it feels." I answered, "Well, as a matter of fact, I do, but it wasn't because of a stand on homosexuality. It was because of a stand on a basketball game." She simply looked confused, and I didn't bother to explain. For anybody to resort to spitting on any occasion is just simply wrong.

It was interesting to find out that I was the second woman sports writer in Texas. I kept thinking I was first but was assured there was one ahead of me. I never did know her name but admire her courage.

I don't know about her, but my days were difficult. Once in Carlsbad, New Mexico, the guard refused to allow me into the press box. I said, "Well, I'll just sit here on the steps and report this game and sell the story to Associated Press about me sitting on the steps." At that point, he went into the press box and asked the "guys" if I was a sports writer. They reluctantly admitted that I was. So, he let me into the press box and sat me behind a post. I would have done better on the steps.

Another time on a snowy night in San Angelo, Texas, I was covering a playoff game in football between Andrews and Brownwood. When they said I couldn't get in out of the snow into the press box, I was most unhappy. I kicked, bucked, and yelled, until I got inside. These tactics actually helped me learn how to later cover news for the Presbyterian Church as news director because sometimes, the dear church folks wanted to keep the press out of the meetings.

When I got into that San Angelo press box, the reporters began to pay each other off; it seems that they were betting on whether or not I would make it. There was a framed set of rules on the wall, and the first rule was: "No ladies in the press box." Oh well, I wasn't much of a lady.

At that game, they were offering another set of wagers on who was going to win state in two different categories. They picked Brownwood and one of the Houston high schools. I said, "Oh no, it will be Refugio and Plano." They asked, "What in the world do you base that prediction upon?" I answered, "Well, Refugio hasn't won in years, and they're hungry to win. Plano is a fast growing, new area, and they've never won so they're eager to win." "Huh," said the reporter, and turned to his friends and laughed, "We're now going on women's intuition." Refugio and Plano won that year. I still haven't collected that bet, and I believe that particular reporter has now gone on to his great reward.

I also covered golf. I remember a very young Ben Crenshaw coming from the University of Texas to a tournament in Andrews. He was dressed in orange slacks, orange shirt, orange shoes, and orange cap. His caddy was dressed in orange. He looked like the Great Pumpkin, but he won.

I covered tennis. Also, I covered track, and I stepped on to the track to get a picture of a 440 yard dash finish. Later, as I left the stadium, one woman sarcastically said, "Did you get a picture of your grandson?"

I covered volleyball. My daughter, Carolyn, was an all-district volleyball player and loved it. In Big Spring, the team went to the state finals, and I rode along in the bus. Their star was Rose Magers, who later played on a second place team in the Olympics for the U.S.A. She was great!

I covered horse races. In Andrews, there was a group that loved to go to the horse races. I ended up with press box passes at Sunland, Ruidosa, La Mesa, and Shreveport Downs. That was a lot of fun, but I found out it was not necessarily the sport of kings.

My son, Jim Bob, went with me, and he learned how to pick the winners from the "poop sheet", even though he wasn't old enough to bet. On a few occasions, we went to Mexico to the dog races, and they didn't care. Anyone could bet.

I remember how devastated he was when one horse that was expected to win had its jaws slit the night before the race. That beautiful horse bled to death in his stable.

Later, when I worked at the Presbyterian church headquarters, a friend, Lois Hall, sent me tickets to the Kentucky Derby every year, and I enjoyed that one. Each of my children came to go to it one time with me since there were only two tickets. They're hard to get. Actually, they are impossible to get. The fanfare and celebration around the race of the roses almost restored my belief in the sport of kings.

But back in Ruidosa one night, Jim Bob and I were walking across the patio at our hotel to go to supper. Two jockeys got in a fight in the patio garden. One had a knife, and I was getting ready to send Jim Bob to get security when the one without a knife took care of it. He reached down in the cactus garden, picked a stick cactus right out of the ground at the roots where there are no thorns, then swung the thorny part of the cactus and hit the second jockey right across the eyes with it. No, it wasn't always the sport of kings, but no sports are.

Nevertheless, I think sports are great, and I enjoyed all of them: basketball, volleyball, football, baseball, track, golf, tennis, and horse racing. I never did get to cover hockey or polo, but I had a pretty solid experience in writing about sports.

A Little More
About My Migrant Kids

My three years of teaching at Shelton Elementary in Odem, Texas, which then had a segregated school for Mexican children, was as rewarding as any three years of my life.

I was teaching there because I had just married C.T. (Tex) Carpenter, Jr., who had come home from the war and completed his degree at Texas A & I. He had started several years before and had a serious interruption in which he fought at D Day, Hertgon Forest, and other notable battles. He had obtained a job teaching Vocational Agriculture at Odem. In those days, the wife always went where the husband got a job, which was alright with me. I had been teaching the year before at Kingsville, directing the high school choir, and the junior high music program. That was while Tex finished college.

I've already mentioned that in Odem, I had an opportunity room part of the time. That group of 49 kids saw 28 of them get to high school and 17 of them finish. None of them would have made it without that room.

Some of them were a little bit mean. I remember one of them cursing me right solidly in Spanish, and I kept him after school to paddle him. The bus left. "How am I going to get home?" he asked. I said, "Carmen, I don't have the slightest idea." He didn't curse me again where I could hear it.

The janitor was my friend. His name was Erasmo, and he would come and tell me if any of the boys carried knives. It was against the rules, but they would get their knives out and show them to each other in the boys' restroom.

One day in class, a student named Doratea kept jerking suddenly in her seat, as though she was about to have a fit. I called her up to my desk. "Is something wrong?" I asked. She leaned over my desk with big, frightened eyes and whispered, "Elogio is sticking me with his knife." You have to realize I was only 21 years old, and Elogio was 19. I slapped the desk and said, "Elogio, bring me your knife—NOW!" He flipped open a switchblade, plunged it into his desk, and said, "Mees, if you want it, come and get it." The classroom gasped. I reached behind me for the paddle which the school allowed me to use in those days; however, I grabbed the playground baseball bat, instead. I started down that aisle with the bat and anger in my eyes. Right before I got to him, Elogio slapped shut his knife and handed it to me and said, "Oh well, if you want it that bad . . ." I have always wondered what would have happened if he hadn't done that. I might have ended up in jail. I still have that knife—keep it by my bedside, as a matter of fact.

It was a major victory for me in that room. He exerted more fear around him than any of the others. He did not graduate, but I got him a job with a butcher shop. The last I knew he owned his own meat market.

A youth named Jesus was not as lucky. Jesus was a gentle boy. He was tall, gangling, lovable, and bashful. He would bring me bouquets of flowers which I think he stole out of peoples' yards as he walked to school. When we had art, he drew beautiful lilies and zinnias with cheap Crayolas. I had one of those pictures framed for many years; it disappeared in one of my moves, regrettably.

One day, he brought me a bunch of radishes. I said, "Where did you get these?" "On the dock," he said. He was referring to the railroad loading area. "Jesus, did you steal these?" I asked. "No, Mees. They see me there, and they look the other way." To him, that meant they gave them to him, and he may have been right.

Long after I moved to West Texas and went to work at newspapers, somebody sent me a news clipping which told of the death of Jesus Aguilar. He was digging a sewer ditch which caved in on him, and he suffocated. I wrote a prize-winning column about a boy who stopped to smell the flowers and should have had a better chance in life than to end up in a sewage ditch.

There was also wonderful Pete Rodriquez who worked at the popcorn machine at the local picture show. Every night, one of the boxes of popcorn held a free ticket. If you got that one, you were a winner. Every time I went to the show, I got the free ticket. Strange coincidence . . . Sometimes I would not use it because I was afraid he would get in trouble.

I would tell many more stories about those wonderful kids who didn't have too good a chance in life. I remember I entered Doratea in the Interscholastic League declamation contest. A Hispanic student had never won. In fact, they hadn't even been entered. I told her to dress in her clean blue jeans and starched white shirt. All of those darling little girls who competed got up in ruffly dresses and declaimed poems, such as "The Boy Stood on the Burning Deck" and "In Flanders Field, the Poppies Grow." Doratea got up and said a simple, little piece, complete with her accent, about "Why I Am Glad to be in America." She won. It was a major victory.

Migrant kids and all children of Mexican heritage finally got a better deal in Texas when Hector Garcia and the LULAC organization pressed for integrated schools and won. Hector was from Mercedes, my hometown. His father sold day-old bread off a cart in the streets during the Depression, but he had strong heritage and named his sons for Montezuman emperors: Hector, Montezuma, Xico, and Cuitlahua. They all grew up to be doctors and lawyers and were very influential in helping the Hispanics in Texas. I'm proud to have gone to school with two of them.

And the Billie Sol Days

I sometimes think of this portion of my life as one long nightmare, but at the time, it was very real.

When I went to work for The Pecos Independent newspaper, they wanted me to be the society editor. I was to get more local news into the paper, which I did. They've never had as much local news in the paper before or since because I had lots of contacts. I led Girl Scout troops, church choirs, belonged to study clubs so I knew all kinds of folks. I knew nearly everybody in Pecos, Texas.

Well, I've already mentioned that my reporting soon slopped over into sports, wrecks, fires, meetings, endless meetings . . . school boards, city councils, county commissioners, PTA, and many more.

By the time we got into the "Estes mestess" (as I used to call it), I was the main contact for people who called in news to our paper.

Our newspaper staff, and especially our editor, Oscar Griffin, and our managing editor, Don Kretsinger, were investigating the Estes' tank transaction records at the courthouse.

Almost everybody in town knew that there was something very, very wrong, but the town was prospering, and it's difficult to fight prosperity.

When Billie Sol first came to town, he was a joke. He wore a derby hat, smack dab straight upon his head; it wasn't a western Stetson or a farmer's straw or a baseball cap, like everybody else wore. It looked out of place. He finally left it on a hat rack at some restaurant, and his friends talked him out of going back to get it. He carried an old battered brief case stuffed to the gills with goodness knows what kind of deeds and records and papers. His empire and power grew rapidly. He was solidly backed by one of the local banks, by the Democrat party, to which he was a big donor, and many individuals.

Billie Sol stories were rampant in town. "He's built a house on top of one of the swimming pools at the former Air Base. That gives him an indoor pool, and he won't let girls and boys swim in it at the same time. They have to take turns." "Billie Sol's built a guest house with gold plumbing. He thinks Harry Truman is coming to see him." "Estes is getting local farmers to sign notes for him to borrow money, and he makes their payments. It's crazy." "Sol has built an office out on the Balmorhea highway. He's fixing it up pretty fancy, and he's hiring a big staff." "Estes got angry at the local undertaker because he was dunning him to pay the funeral costs of one of Estes' workers for whom he had ordered a big funeral. So now he's bought the old Ross house and is going to put in an elaborate funeral parlor and try to run the current undertaker out of business." "Billie Sol seems to be getting extra cotton acreage allotment from the Agriculture Conservation Service by getting eminent domain acreage (highway right-of-ways, lake right-of-ways, and others)." "Sol has invited somebody from Washington's Agriculture Department to speak at the Chamber banquet. He seems to know everybody." "Estes has been named as one of the ten outstanding young men in the nation by the Jaycees. He is listed along with the Governor of Tennessee and several others. Security State Bank is having a big barbecue for him." "Billie Sol has dyed the grass in his front yard green and planted three palm trees. Palms don't grow in West Texas. I also hear he has a monkey in a cage in his living room. Is that crazy or what?"

Now, my husband and I didn't agree on many things in those hectic days, but we did agree that Estes was destroying our community. Tex came home from work one day and said, "I got in trouble at the bank today." It was right after Estes had been named outstanding young man in the nation. Estes had come through the bank door at the rear of the bank right after closing time and demanded service. Everybody began to fall all over themselves trying to help him. He purchased an $8,000 cashier's check at Ruth Ligon's cage. My husband's teller cage was right next to it. After Estes got his check, he started talking to somebody and absent-mindedly tore the check into pieces and dropped the scraps on the floor. Suddenly, he was looking for the check and asked Ruth, "Where's my check?" Ruth answered calmly, "I think you tore it up, and it's on the floor." "Write me another," he demanded. "I need the number off of that one,' she answered. Whereupon he knelt on the floor and started putting the check back together. My husband is reported to have leaned out of his cage and said, "I call that pretty damned outstanding." My husband was scolded severely by bank officials.

It was that same week that my husband and I drove one night to pick up five dinners for our family. We went to Ben's Spanish Inn. They had great Mexican food, and we ate there a lot. I'd called in our order, and we drove by to pick it up. Unfortunately, Billie Sol and I got to the cash register at the same time. "Give me Marj's ticket," said the magnanimous Estes. "No, thank you," I said, thinking how horrified my husband would be. We argued briefly. Used to getting his way, Sol turned to Mrs. Mata at the register, "If you don't take my money for her food, I'll not trade here again." She looked at me pitifully. I said, "Fine." I took my food and walked out without saying thank you. And yes, my husband did have a fit.

I remember another story. One Christmas season, Estes hosted the entire Junior High band with a sit-down Christmas dinner in his huge living room. Some of his daughters and one of my daughters were in that band. Our newspaper staff was having their Christmas party that same night, and during the course of the evening, they bet me that I wouldn't go to the Estes house and take a news picture of the dinner for our paper. I said, "Put your money on the table," and off I went. When I got to the door, Estes had a new butler. He saw the camera and thought I was from Estes' newspaper. "Come in. You are late," he said. I marched into the living room, and the kids seemed to be collectively holding their breaths. Everybody in town knew about the news war. I went up to the head table and took a picture of Estes. Then, I took a picture of the crowd and hastily started walking out of there. I heard him mincing along behind me. When I got to the foyer, he said, "Wait here." I thought, "Oh, my gosh. What now?" He came back with three packages of frozen beef: a roast and T-bones. He said piously, "I love my enemies. Merry Christmas." Well, I fled back to the party. I said, "I got a picture, and I got T-bones." And I picked up the money. "Don't eat those steaks," Oscar said. But I did. And later I sold a picture taken that night of Estes to Fortune Magazine. We had not used that picture at our paper. We used the one of the crowd. The following June, when Fortune was doing a story some two months after his arrest on March 29, 1962, they wanted a picture of him that had not been used and that was a little bit different. I offered them the picture of Billie Sol in his checked sports coat sitting in front of a potted palm at the band dinner. They offered me "seven fifty." I thought $7.50 was pretty cheap but said, "O.K., if I get a credit line." They agreed and sent me a check for $750.00. I was stunned. And I got the credit line at the end of the article in very small print where it says: "M. Carpenter. Pecos Independent".

I remember later when he had been arrested and was out on bail. The family decided to move to Abilene, and they moved in the middle of the night. Now you have to pay right well to get two moving vans to come to your house at night. Pat Ryan, who worked in our advertising department, called me and said, "Billie Sol is moving out. Grab a camera." We drove to Estes' house and drove in the alley and took a picture of the van in the alley moving things out the back door. Then we drove around to the front and daringly went right up in the driveway; I was standing in the middle of the yard getting a picture of the van out front when they turned on the sprinkler system. I was drenched, and Pat was laughing so hard he could hardly get the car backed out of the driveway.

All the stories and rumors were not fun or funny. Billie Sol ran for the school board, and Don Kretsinger refused to take money for ads to endorse him and came out against him on the editorial page.

We heard later that Estes was vying for becoming Secretary of Agriculture and had been told he needed to win a local election. The paper endorsed the write-in campaign of Bill Mattox. It's difficult to win on a write-in vote, but Mattox won.

And There Were Bad Days

Billie Sol took a dim view of that election loss. He had planned a victory barbecue that turned into a wake. That's the day that he became so angry that he decided to start a newspaper of his own and try to run us out of business. Thereby, he set off the tackiest news war in West Texas history. He offered classified ads for 25 cents. He contacted all of our major advertisers and undercut us "big time". He hired paper boys to go out in town and pick up our newspaper in the yards of our subscribers and put his down free. His editor wrote a front page editorial calling me Judas and said that I got 800 pieces of silver (he didn't know his Bible) for corresponding for Associated Press and many of the large Texas dailies, as well as furnishing help to Life magazine, Time magazine, and the New York newspapers.

The day that the editorial came out, I got in the newspaper car and drove to every news stand in town, removed all of their papers, and tossed them in the trash. When they went back the next day to collect, they were told, "There's no money in the coin box. Marj came and took all of the papers away; we didn't really blame her and didn't try to stop her."

It was scary times. I remember walking into the newspaper office one night after taking pictures. The office was locked. I unlocked the door and stepped back because the building was full of gas. If I'd been one of the staff who smoked (and most of them did in those days), I would have been blown away. I went outside to telephone and called the fire department who came and turned off the gas. We had a big iron pot in which we melted hot lead. It had a pilot light which was constantly burning. Somebody knew that and knew how to turn it off from outside in the alley. They turned the gas off and of course, the pilot went out. Then, they turned the gas back on and of course, there was nobody there to light it.

Another night I went to the paper late after I'd covered the basketball banquet at the high school. The back of the newspaper office was on fire, and the place was filled with smoke. Again, I was Paul Revere and got the fire department. Somebody had poured gasoline on the back door and thrown a torch on the roof. The gasoline can was still sitting in the alley.

I remember that Levi Garret, who at that time was a member of the city council, said to me, "I'm not surprised you had a fire with all that trash in the alley and the wind blowing." To which I quipped, "Oh, I know that. We have cans of gasoline blow down our alley all the time."

One funny incident happened in our alley. Both our newspaper and Sol's newspaper had the kind of equipment in which they punched out tapes similar to the method of the old player pianos. They then ran them through to print out our stories.

We suddenly realized that the opposition paper was sometimes running stories that we had written, word for word, before we could get them in our publication. They printed every day, and we came out only twice a week. We figured out that they had to be stealing tapes out of our trash box in the alley. So we watched for them. I still remember Furd Love slamming the lid and trapping a guy inside the trash. The man was yelling and kicking, and Furd was screaming, "Call the police, and tell them they're stealing our trash." Of course, that sounded pretty ridiculous, and the police didn't like us much anyway so we didn't call. We just shredded our tapes from that point on. Oh yes, we let him out of the trash box, and he ran away.

Speaking of the police, the department was officially on the Estes side of that news war; however, some of the individual police liked us and would try to help us. Look Magazine played a dirty trick on the chief of police. Fletcher Knoebel had written an article called "The Kind of Town That Produced Billie Sol Estes". The mayor and a banker later sued the magazine but ended up settling out of court and paying all the court costs.

When the Look magazine photographer came to town, he tricked the chief. He asked him to pose in front of the post office building and then kept urging him to, "Step a little to the left, please; there is better light." They maneuvered him into a spot where he unknowingly stood by a city trash can with the words painted on the side, "Please Help Keep Our City Clean". A lot of people got a chuckle out of that picture.

That news war nearly destroyed a community full of good people who were caught up in fear, hate, anger, and confusion. The Estes scandal was followed by a second scandal, involving doctors of the community and the hospital. It was too much. It affected individual families, schools, churches, and businesses. Like children, we got up every morning, chose up sides, and started a new fight.

It's not a time of life that I remember with great joy because so many lives were affected, but I do try to remember the funny times.

One of those was when my daughter, Carolyn, came peddling home on her bike all out of breath. With great pride she handed me a brick which had painted on it, "Read the Pecos Daily News." (which was Estes' paper). It was a windy West Texas day. When Carolyn took that brick off a huge stack of their newspapers in front of the Stop and Shop, those papers took off and blew all up and down Eddy Street. She and I sat down and laughed when she told me.

After Billie Sol was arrested, I met all kinds of folks. George and Barbara Bush came over from Midland for information for the Republican Party. That's the first time I met a Bush. Later, I met George W. and Laura, as well.

In 1962 reporters came from all over the place, even newspapers in Europe. It was the story of the year in the United States. Some twenty years later, when I was news director for the Presbyterian Church (USA) the religion story of the year was the release of the homosexuality report by a committee and then the big vote against it at the church's General Assembly in Baltimore. I really don't know of any other reporter that has been involved in both the secular story of the year in the nation and the Religion News Writers' story of the year in the nation, but there may be another one out there somewhere. I've learned never to say "only" about anything or anyone.

I well remember when a young Dan Rather came to Pecos during the Estes days. He had just been hired by CBS from a Houston television station. I was filmed with him for the six o'clock news. I was a little perturbed because they told me in advance what the questions would be and suggested answers. I was to lean casually on the counter at the front of the news office. As we began, they kept saying, "Look at Dan. Look at Dan. Look at Dan." I wasn't all that excited about it. As we started the interview, they started over with the "Look at Dan" routine. They asked the first question, "Why did The Pecos Independent decide to go after Billie Sol Estes?" My answering sentence was to begin with, "Actually . . ." Suddenly, They screamed, "Stop! Stop! Stop! Turn off that noisy air conditioner." So our news staff now was sitting and sweating. We started again, and they asked that same question. As I answered, "Actually . . ." they screamed, "Stop! Stop! Stop! Cease those noisy typewriters." So now the staff was sitting, sweating, and idle. The third time they asked it, I answered, "Actually, I no longer remember what in the world I'm supposed to say." And they screamed out how much I had just cost the network for the delay; I answered, "So did you . . . twice."

We finally got the few questions completed. On that very night, Billie Sol's friends in Pecos bought his newspaper, so they could continue its publication. We were crushed. As I went to work the next morning, Dan Rather was sitting on the fender of a car out front of the news office. "Hi, Marj," he said, "You won." I looked at him in disdain and said, "Won what? Dan Rather, you don't have the slightest idea what's going on here." I have to admit I included a couple expletives. As it turned out, it was our newspaper that had to eventually shut down. We lost that night. We won nothing.

Years later, when I was selected by Carol Weir to handle the press for the returning of Hostage Ben Weir, we held the opening press conference at the National Presbyterian Church in Washington, D.C. We had agreed and set up an interview after the press conference with CBS in the back of the church with Dan Rather. It was to be included in his newscast. I asked that they keep the lights on Weir as short a time as possible because he had been captive in the dark for many months, and his eyes were weak. The interview went fine, and then Dan kept questioning him afterward. I knew the filming was over, but the lights remained on. I kept saying, "Lights, lights," and everybody ignored me, so I unplugged them. Then, the union workers went crazy. Everybody was screaming at me, including Dan. I said, "Dan Rather, you still don't have the slightest idea what's going on." And I included those same expletives. "Have I met you before?" he asked. I answered, "Oh yes, twenty-five years ago—Pecos, Texas, 1962."

That wonderful week of handling Weir's press proved that church news could also be exciting. He was interviewed by many major publications, as well as by Tom Brokaw, Peter Jennings, MacNeal Layer, Larry King, and all three morning shows.

I've never, ever had a dull job—never.

The Camera and I

"I hear Estes is starting a daily newspaper and getting together top equipment so he can run The Pecos Independent out of business." This was told to me in an anonymous phone call.

And he certainly tried. Even though it was a small town, it turned into one of the fiercest of news wars in history.

When I went to work for the paper, I had taken lots of pictures on a candid camera, but that's a lot different from news photography.

Oscar Griffin had been taking most of the pictures for the paper, and he had a good eye for a photo. When I came along and began to ask him to take more and more news and society pictures, he decided to teach me to use the old 4x5 camera so that he didn't have to attend all the many events.

You've seen those old cameras in the ancient black and white movies where they show reporters with a press card stuck in the brim of their hats and a big camera in their hand with flash bulbs and film holder in a camera case. The film holder slid in and out of a slot in the camera.

I had some hilarious experiences with that camera. Early on, they sent me to the Country Club to a style show. Oscar sure didn't want to go to that. When I got there, I had lost my ticket. I looked everywhere and couldn't find it, but they decided to admit me anyway because they wanted pictures in the paper.

Later, when the dark room developer was developing my fashion shots, he came out and told Oscar, "Marj is getting clever. She put her ticket at an angle inside one of the holders and got a great shot of a model with the ticket angled across her." I opened my mouth to protest and then decided to be quiet and act like I really was clever.

That camera, unlike smaller models of news cameras which came along later, could double expose. One night at a football game I was taking pictures. I shot a halftime exposure of the drum major leading the band. I forgot to change sides of the holder. So the photograph also had the football team running down the field for the kickoff of the second half. We ran it as "The Spirit of Football." It was a prize winner.

I never did conquer the dark room. I left that to the experts. When I won a national news photography contest and they wrote and asked what "f stop" I used and what type of developer in the darkroom, I turned the form over to the editor to fill out and answer.

The winning picture was a winner simply because I was at the right place at the right time, as is often the case. We were ambulance chasing reporters. We tried to get everywhere ahead of our "Estes competition." One day I raced behind the ambulance and fire truck out to a small private airfield. There was a crop dusting pilot trying to land his small, open plane. He had struck the edge of an irrigation ditch while flying low over a cotton field and knocked off a wheel. So he was now trying to land with only one wheel. A crash was expected. He kept flying low over the field. I pointed the camera and got a great shot of the plane with one wheel. He was so close that I caught the pilot's distressed face. He landed without getting hurt, and we ran the picture as "Coming in on a Wheel and a Prayer".

Another great picture that I shot was several years later in Andrews, Texas. Again, I followed the fire truck. It pulled up to a house and then left. "No fire." Something made me stay and get out of the car. There was still a police car there. In a moment, a policeman came out of the house carrying a baby wrapped in a blanket. Two children walking through the yard to go home from school were looking up at the policeman. He had saved a baby whom they thought had drowned in the bathtub. It was another prize-winning shot.

I surely don't want you to think all of my photographs were winners. I took hundreds of bummers. My third favorite was another Billie Sol Estes shot. His first trial was attempted in Pecos, Texas, And moved on a change of venue to a state court in Tyler, Texas, where he was found guilty on several charges of fraud and sentenced.

Then, he was to be tried again in federal court in El Paso. I rode the Greyhound bus to El Paso from Pecos to cover the trial. That's over 375 miles. I carried my big, old camera in my lap. I was dressed up, for me, in an outfit topped with a new red coat, and I wore high heeled shoes. I took a taxi straight to federal court. I was late. I had to check my camera at the door, and I was hustling down the aisle, hoping for a seat in the press section which was quite full. Luckily for me, Judge Thomason, who often presided over federal court in Pecos, recognized me and turned to the press section and said, "Here comes a lady in red who works for the paper that started this case. Will one of the press please give her a front row seat?" Bless him. They did.

It got more interesting at noon. I checked my camera back out and stood outside the courthouse waiting for Billie Sol to come back from lunch. I skipped lunch. I needed a news photo. The problem was that there was more than one way back to the courthouse and more than one way into the building. Some of the nationally known reporters decided to help this poor country gal out. They kept lookouts in different streets. Suddenly a Life magazine reporter called out, "Marj, here he comes." I turned and began to run in that direction. I snapped the heel off my right shoe so I was bobbing up and down ridiculously. Billie Sol, one of his brothers, his father, and his uncle were all crossing the street at the traffic light in a row like tin soldiers. They all swung their arms and legs out in unison. They all turned to look toward that great red blob dancing up and down, and I shot the picture. Associated Press later ran it as "the Estes parade." It was a very lucky shot.

It was real progress when they bought a "strobe unit", which we used instead of flash bulbs on the camera. My children were glad because they used to recall that The Pecos Independent car that I drove had crushed flashbulbs and blackened flashbulbs rolling around on the back floor.

One time when we got caught in a West Texas hail storm, I urged Jim Bob to lie down on the back floorboard. He asked, "Is it worse to get hit by hail or cut up by flashbulbs?"

There was one night in Pecos that I went to seven different events and took pictures. This was with the four by five camera. I put the holders that I had already used on the front seat of my car and went in to take an eighth picture. When I came out of that event, all of the slides in the car seat had been pulled out and the pictures exposed and ruined. My entire evening's work was wiped out. I returned to five of the events and retook pictures. It was too late for the other two. I was shaking with anger. Then I remembered, "Don't get mad. Get even."

Billie Sol's paper took the Associated Press daily wire service. We couldn't afford it and only got mail-in features. They had daily news pouring in at their paper.

I had been covering the complicated Agriculture Cotton Hearings for Associated Press. They didn't even understand them at the other paper. The hearings involved Estes and several area farmers. I had called the story in to A.P. I knew it would come out in the wire service of the Daily News, and they had the right to use it.

That night I was so angry that I walked in their front door boldly and stood in front of the A.P. teletype. When my story came in, I ripped it off and walked out the door and drove home.

Ross McSwain, a reporter at a nearby daily paper, The San Angelo Standard Times, for whom I corresponded, telephoned me at home. He was laughing. He said, "The Pecos Daily News is saying on the A.P. wire that you stole their cotton allotment story, and they want it rerun." A.P. had told them, "Well, she wrote it." Then they added that they were bogged down with news and couldn't run it again for another two hours. So the rival paper had to stay up two hours so they could run the story the next day, minus my byline. But I had a good laugh.

We were like children in a mud fight. Nothing was too petty to try.

I had many other photo experiences as I changed and began to use more modern cameras—no more holders and no more flashbulbs. But you did have to remember to keep the camera loaded and the battery charged, and you needed to keep the camera within reach.

One time in Andrews, Texas, somebody else had used my camera unbeknownst to me and didn't reload it. I arrived at a 2 A.M. fatal wreck before realizing that I had an empty camera. Never mind what I said.

I recall another wreck outside Andrews. It was a single vehicle rollover. The woman driver was thrown out and unconscious. She regained partial consciousness in the hospital and kept reaching for a baby. We rushed back to the scene. A fourteen-month old baby was sitting under a mesquite bush happily stuffing dirt in his mouth. Incredible.

That's what made newspaper reporting interesting. You never knew what would happen next.

Second Section

How Did I Get to Be Like This?

Contents

Mama Knows Best 47

But Daddy Had More Fun 51

A Brother and a Sister 55

About Grandmothers 58

And About Grandpas 61

Everybody Needs One 66

About Storms, Bananas, and Red Bicycles 69

About Cheese Sandwiches 72

Speaking of the Famous 74

Sometimes It Was Funny 78

Who Else Is Famous? 82

The Chapter That I Hate 86

Mama Knows Best

And in our family, this was definitely true. My Mama was of Pennsylvania Dutch stock, moved to Texas when she was eight years old, and was intelligent, caring, loving, and tough.

She did not have an easy life. Her father took the family down the Mississippi in 1908 in a boat, on to Galveston, overland to South Texas where her mother immediately took malaria, a flood came, and they lived in the newly-built barn while the flood washed away the lumber for the house.

But they saved their automobile which had also gone down the Mississippi on the boat from Philadelphia and had carried them to South Texas via wagon trails and railroad tracks.

They survived all of that tragedy and more. When Mama was a senior in high school, the Cavalry came to the Mercedes area on the Rio Grande River of Texas in the Mexican bandit wars. The Presbyterian Church held an ice cream supper for the soldier boys in the yard of the Diehl's (my mother's maiden name) home. Mother met Walter Collier, one of the soldiers, and later they married; however, they didn't marry as much later as her parents would have preferred. She was an excellent student, and they had planned for her to return back East and go to college. But she and Walter married, and she went with him to Chattanooga where he was briefly stationed with the army before going overseas in World War I. She stayed with his parents in Hornell, New York, since her father was no longer speaking to her.

But by the end of the war, they worked that out, and everybody was speaking again. Her husband was due to come home on a troop ship, and he was on the dock at Le Harve in France, getting ready to board, when they pulled him and six other regular army guys aside. They told them they were to remain in France to hunt down deserters. He was devastated and extremely upset so he did not write home or communicate in any way for weeks.

In the meantime, Mother met the ship and waited until every soldier had disembarked while bands played happily and ticker tape fell. He was not there. She looked and looked and cried and cried. She wrote the War Department four times before he was finally traced and told to write home. Needless to say, there was some fence mending to do when he did arrive home.

He was next assigned to Amhurst University in Massachusetts. The army put him in charge of what would now be an ROTC unit. After they had been there several months, the University officials called him in at midterm and told him that he must move because he was living in the Irish part of town. They said that you could not teach at Amhurst and live there. This made him very angry because he was Irish.

So, instead of re-enlisting in the army, he asked for a discharge. Mother objected, but he got one anyway. They then returned to Mercedes where her father (who was tired of working anyway) gave his garage to his son, Harvey, and his son-in-law, Walter, to run. And they ran it. Harvey very soon sold out his part and joined the Border Patrol, thinking it was more exciting.

Things rocked along for several years with Dad building a clientele. Then, the hurricane of 1933 struck the Rio Grande Valley and killed over eighty persons. The roof of that garage was blown off, and it cut right down through the middle of the building. The morning after the storm ended, my Mama, her mother, and we two kids walked to town in the rain. The two women decided to rent an empty store on 3rd Street (it was Depression years and there were a lot of empty stores) and start a car parts business.

They took the tires, batteries, and car parts from the garage and began that business. That business thrived for my parents and carried them through to their retirement. By then, they had built their own store. Mother and Dad ran the store, but Mother really ran it. She studied parts catalogues and became an expert on car parts. Mechanics and garage owners came from all over the Valley to buy parts from her. She never did neglect home during those years.

There never was a better cook—Pennsylvania Dutch, no less. There never was a better seamstress. She made all my clothes for years, including silk-lined, tailored suits and beautiful formals. She later made sister dresses for my daughters.

She tried to teach me to sew. It was hopeless. I even sewed one dress together with the seams on the outside. She never did really teach me to cook because she didn't like anybody in her kitchen while she was cooking. But she shared her recipes with me later, and I did the best I could—but I never matched her cooking expertise.

She taught the young people's class at the church and kept up with her kids as they went into adulthood. She sang in the choir. She held the Easter Egg hunts for the Sunday school in her yard. She loved the church.

She also loved her family, but she didn't have much patience with any other kind of entertaining. She didn't have any more time. She kept the bank accounts and made all the major decisions.

She decided when we were to buy a car. She decided when we could take a trip. She paid all bills in cash, including a new car. She backed me to the hilt in every project I ever undertook, and was encouraging. If I failed at something, she seemed to suffer with me.

I guess one of her biggest disappointments is that I went to a manse to get married by the preacher and then called and told her. She would have loved to have put on a big wedding. But that was a decision I made because my husband-to-be's mother said she would not come to a wedding. That would have been a mess. So we just got married in a college town. He went back to class and took an exam the next morning. I had already graduated at that time.

But my Mama accepted that and came to his graduation when his own Mother did not appear. Mama came and helped when my babies were born. She went to elaborate pains at Christmas to be sure everybody got everything they could want. When my parents would drive to West Texas at Christmas, the kids said it was like Santa Claus' sleigh arrived.

She enjoyed life, but not openly. I only remember her really laughing hard a few times in her life. One time, I was squirting Cool Whip (a new product then) on the pumpkin pie at Christmas. It got out of control and went all over the ceiling, the window, and on to the turkey. She did laugh.

I remember once being with her when we were riding behind a woman in a very fancy convertible who was one of the most arrogant women in the community. We stopped behind her at a traffic light. She had stopped behind a cement truck. Suddenly, the cement truck began to pour concrete all over the front of the convertible, and the woman jumped out and was screaming, screeching, and cursing. And Mother did laugh.

My daughter, Carolyn, tells me that when she went to see her Grandmother one summer, it turned out to be the week before she died. Carolyn told Grandma a story about herself and her sister, Cathy, going "pony-trekking" in Wales. Cathy wasn't an expert horsewoman, to put it mildly. She came bouncing out on a horse with the saddle sideways and was squealing and hollering. As Carolyn told it, Grandma laughed and laughed.

Mama had a sad life. She lost two of her three children before they were grown. She lost her Mother young. They lost their first business in a storm.

But she had a happy life. She loved and supported her husband. She was proud of my children and of me. She ran a successful business. She dedicated herself to the church. She was a caring, loving mother, and she was smart. Her decisions were almost always right. Mama did know best.

But Daddy Had More Fun

While my practical mother kept the house and the business and the family going, my Dad had fun. And he made fun for others, as well.

This happy-go-lucky Irishman is the person who taught me to love to travel. He taught me to love people. He taught me to care about the underdog. In fact, if he thought somebody was really in need, he would give him the shirt off his back, unless Mama got hold of the shirt tail first.

He was extremely helpful to youth and was often named father of the year. He taught marksmanship to Boy Scouts and was named a Silver Beaver. He started the first Hispanic scout troop in South Texas.

He gave hours and hours raising money for Little League and Pony League and spent more hours coaching the teams. He especially emphasized that the many Hispanic children in South Texas had a chance to play.

The Little League Park in that town was named the Walter Collier Park. Since it was under urban renewal funds, they said it couldn't be named for anybody who was living. So they named it Kennedy Park. The day Dad died, they renamed it Walter Collier Park. The week before he died they presented him a bat marked Walter Collier, Batting Average with Youth: 1000.

When the school had no school buses, he got the cars together to take the football team to the games. He also gathered the cars for the band. I never did know who got the cars for the pep squad.

I remember one game my senior year, when Mission High School beat us 20-0. They won the championship. One player in Mission—a kid named Tom Landry—made all 20 points. We said ugly things about him all the way home. But we later praised him when he coached the Dallas Cowboys.

Dad was extremely patriotic. He had served in the Mexican bandit days and in World War I, when he was among those "mustard gassed". This bothered him most of his life, but he added to the botheration by smoking two packs of cigarettes a day.

He had been cited for bravery during the bandit days when he and three other soldiers and two Texas rangers laid behind the railroad track at Norias Switch on the King Ranch and protected the ranch from the invading Pancho Villa. He also went along with General Pershing down into Mexico chasing Villa. They got cut off down there and on one particular Christmas Day had only three spoonfuls of beans for dinner. We heard that story every Christmas right before the prayer before dinner. Dad also served in France and as I mentioned earlier, remained behind to pick up deserters.

So, he had no patience with those who were not patriotic. On the day after Pearl Harbor Day, he tried to rejoin the army. They wouldn't have him. So, he sold Defense Bonds, collected scrap metal, and even briefly served as an air raid warden when they thought Japan was going to come up through Mexico and bomb Texas.

He also was a tire inspector, since he sold tires. During the war, you were only allowed to sell tires to those whose tires were "plumb worn out". Many people tried to pay under the counter to get new tires. One day a man offered Dad money for approval for his tires. Dad hit him and knocked him out of the front door of the store into the street. It turned out that he had struck a government agent checking to see if the tire inspectors were honest. No government man ever approached Dad again. That agent must have turned in a full report on my Dad. I only ever knew of one other person who questioned my Father's honesty. Dad was Sunday School superintendent, and once a year, he put together a picnic where all of us went to McAllen to Cascade Swimming Pool. It was the party of the year for us. He raised the money for it. He was on the sidewalk on Main Street one day when one fellow who was a member of the church accused him of taking the money from the offering. He hit that man, too, and the guy fought back. They both got taken to the city jail. I've never seen my Mother so angry as when she went to get him out of jail.

In 1936, my Dad took my brother and I to the Texas Centennial in Dallas. I had never been out of the Rio Grande Valley. I was ten, and my brother was twelve. In the Valley, the towns touched each other, and when we started across that King Ranch, I was frightened. I thought we were going to the end of the earth.

But we got to San Antonio and saw the Alamo and the zoo and all those wonderful things. We got to Dallas and saw the Centennial which had fake dinosaurs and free orange juice and fireworks.

We went on to Raton, New Mexico, where my Father had run away from home when he was seventeen to join the Cavalry. He had overheard his parents wondering how a railroad worker's salary was going to keep providing enough food for those six kids. So, he decided he was the oldest boy and that if he left, there would only be five kids.

He never went past the eighth grade. But I have never known a better read person. He read Shakespeare and O. Henry and Wordsworth and all kinds of books. He read the Bible. In his golden years, he regressed to paper backs, but he never quit reading.

A funny thing happened on the way home from that trip. We were south of San Antonio in the home stretch, and we kept seeing watermelon stands by the side of the road. Outside Floresville, Dad stopped at a stand where a teen-aged youth was selling watermelons. Dad bought one, cut it in half, and told my brother and I to go after it. We each ate a half watermelon. He figured if we got sick, we were going to be home by night. What is really the strangest thing about this story happened later. Ten years later, after the war, I met C.T. (Tex) Carpenter from Floresville, home from Europe where he served from D Day until it was over. We married that year. One day I told the watermelon story, and he was stunned. He said, "That was me selling the watermelons. It was 1936. This man drove up, cut a watermelon in half, and gave it to his little girl and boy. They made a mess." I said, "Well, that shows you need to be careful who you sell watermelons to . . ."

My brother died in 1937, and in 1939, Dad decided that he and I should go to New York and meet his parents and brothers and sisters and then, go to the World's Fair. Mother refused to go. She hated to travel, but we did it. It was the most marvelous trip. I fished on the Finger Lakes. I picked blueberries. I rolled on hills of daisies. I went to the Fair. I rode the tallest roller coaster I have ever seen and lost my new straw hat. It blew away. I went to Washington, D.C. I went to Gettysburg. I went to Somerset, Kentucky, where my Dad had once lived. I went to Chicago.

I went to Cincinnati where years later I was elected moderator of the Presbyterian Church, U.S.A. I went to New Orleans. And I went home, bitten by the travel bug, full of stories, happy, tired, and smarter than I was when I left.

Years later in 1964, my Dad sent me a check to get on the train and take that same trip with my three children and take them to the New York World's Fair. I told him I needed the money for their college coming up, because my husband was out of work, and my salary was poor. He said, "We didn't have any money in 1939 either. But we went. You either use the check to go to the Fair or send it back." We went to the Fair, and it was wonderful. We went to Washington, D. C. We went to Chicago. We went to Cincinnati. We went to New York City and to the shows on Broadway. We went to New Orleans, and we went home, happy, tired, and smarter than when we left.

Thank you, Daddy. You made me love travel. You made me love people. And I sure loved you.

A Brother and a Sister

There is nothing more lonely than being an only child—except being an only child after your brother and your sister have died. Expectations from your parents run very high.

My sister, Beatrice, died when she was four years old, shortly before I was born. I heard the story over and over. After the noon meal, she ran out in the front yard to play. The family heard a scream and went out in time to see that a stray horse had kicked her in the head, and her head had then hit a rock. She went into a coma for thirty days and then died.

My father, who had been in the cavalry and loved horses, shot that horse on the spot. Nobody ever claimed the dead horse. Needless to say, I did not grow up into a Texan who loved horses.

When I was born, early pictures of Beatrice and I show that we were very similar in looks, but I often overheard from parents, grandparents, and friends, "But Beatrice had such a sweet, loving disposition." Oh, well.

My brother, Walter, was two years younger than Beatrice and two years older than me. He and I were very close. We did everything together. Now, he really did have a sweet disposition. I never was accused of that—even to this day.

I remember when he was in the first grade, they let the students each bring a guest on visitor's day. He took me along as his guest. He was the only one who brought a child. I still remember that he put his arm around my shoulder and introduced me to everyone with great pride. We played cowboys together. We went to church and Sunday School together.

We went to the beach on holidays together. We joined the school band together. We were inseparable.

My Grandpa had given him a beautiful watch fob, but he didn't have a watch. I was saving nickels and dimes to buy him a pocket watch for Christmas when he died in November.

He was a freshman in high school. He became very ill, and my parents took him to Scott and White Hospital in Temple, Texas, considered the best in the state. He never returned. He had Bright's disease—kidney failure, and there was no dialysis treatment or kidney transplants in 1937.

One of my happiest memories of him was when we were small and some kids ran through our field and said, "Lindberg is in the floodway!" We never questioned it. We ran to the levee and down to the flat floodway where, sure enough, Lindberg had landed his little plane to check on the engine and was doing so. We all watched in awe. He shook every hand and patted every head and flew away. There were no adults there. Walter always wanted to be a Lindberg after that.

Walter and I always walked home from school together, except one day. I had a "C" on my straight "A" report card and told him I wasn't going home. I sat on the school steps until the sun went down, and my father came and got me.

Another time when Walter was in the third grade, two boys from his class jumped him in an alley. He fought, and I fought. A boy named Raymond stuck me headfirst into a trash can. I came out of there throwing trash—bottles, cans, and paper. The school principal saw us in the alley and stopped the fight and told us to pick up the trash. We couldn't get the coffee grounds and lettuce leaves picked up. I learned something that day that later helped me in the news world. When you dig out all the garbage on any issue, you can't get it all back in the can.

There are few things in life that make me go to pieces. I'm usually pretty calm. But there are two related to the memory of Walter's dying that really upset me. He had played a French horn in the band, and the band played "Nearer My God to Thee" at the cemetery. Hearing that hymn does me in every time.

When they had taken Walter to Temple, I was left at the home of my friend, Joyce Clarke. Word had come to the Clarke's that my brother had died, and Mrs. Clarke was trying to decide whether to tell me or wait for my parents who were in route home. Unfortunately, Joyce's little brother, Kenneth, was about nine years old, and he had overheard his mother talking. Then, he yelled at me as I was walking across the

canal bridge to their home, "Your brother is dead. Your brother died."
I didn't believe it, but when Joyce told her Mother what had happened,
Mrs. Clarke called me aside and told me. Then we went into supper,
and she served potato soup. Please don't ever serve me potato soup.
It sticks in my throat every time.

Then, as I went on into high school, there were great demands on me,
"Your mother was valedictorian. We hope you will be." I was. "There's an
award this year for outstanding senior. We hope you get it." I did.

"You've done so well with your piano music. We hope you'll major in
music in college." I did. But my heart was in journalism. I worked with
journalism voluntarily in college and became the only music major who
edited the college newspaper.

My parents didn't mean to be over-demanding. They had lost so much,
and their hopes were pinned on me.

It made me a hopeless workaholic, but I'm thankful because that has
caused me to have an interesting life.

About Grandmothers

My two grandmothers were very influential in the way I have turned out.

My Grandma Diehl (whom I always referred to simply as Grandma) lived across the field from us until she died, when I was just six years old. But oh, the impact she had in those six years. I always wanted to please her. I dearly loved her. Sundays were special because after church and Sunday School we went to her house and ate chicken. It was always chicken because it was the Depression years, and they had chickens. Sometimes it was fried chicken. Sometimes it was baked chicken and dressing. Sometimes it was stewed chicken and dumplings.

After dinner (we called the noon meal dinner), everyone would rest, and then Grandma would take my brother, Walter, and me to the barn. We would sit with her in the swing. She told us about missionaries. And she read us Bible stories. And she read from the Bible itself.

One Sunday I asked why we couldn't read something else . . . and she answered, "Because Sunday is the Lord's Day." And that was that.

We always ate slices of apple and Saltine crackers while she read or talked. To this day, whenever I happen to eat apples and crackers together, I am back in that swing.

I was in the first grade when she died. Whatever she was suffering from, she refused to go to the hospital for surgery. I think it was a ruptured appendix. She died at home. My Dad came to the first grade and third grade to get Walter and me to see her shortly before she died.

I had been laboriously working on an oven potholder made out of colored rags as a gift for my mother for Christmas. This was in late

November, and Mrs. Lyle (our first grade teacher) knew it would take most of us until Christmas to finish such a project. Mine was lumping all up and was not working right, and I began to cry. My Dad thought I was crying about Grandma, but I didn't even realize there was anything much wrong with Grandma. I was crying about the potholder. But we went to her bedside. A big antique dresser by the bed held a little china purple lady. You could lift her head and skirt and place a pin or button or coin underneath. I always played with it when I got the chance. I kissed Grandma. Then I went over and began to play with the little purple lady. Grandma looked at Grandpa and said, "When I'm gone, give Marjorie the lady." She paused and then added, "And give her the dresser as well."

That request was nearly the undoing of Grandpa. The day after her funeral, he put that heavy dresser on a cotton sack and dragged it across the field. For that effort, he obtained a hernia which was with him the rest of his life—which was another forty years.

But we still have the dresser in our family. And I still have the purple lady. But more than that, I have the memory of Grandma who instilled in me a love for the church and a love for mission.

She did not, however, instill in me a love for chicken, although hers was good. But since I've been on the church circuit, I've had about all of the chicken I ever really wanted.

The other grandmother, I always called "Grandma Collier". She lived far away in Hornell, New York. I received letters and cards and gifts from her but did not meet her until I was twelve years old. There wasn't any extra money for travel in our household. But when I did meet her, I recognized how much like her I was. I inherited genes from Grandma Collier.

Needless to say, she was a character. She loved music. She loved the family. She was one heck of a disciplinarian. If one of the grandchildren kicked her in the shins, she kicked them back. If anyone complained about the food on the table, she said, "It's just the way I like it. And I cooked it."

The last day of her life in 1955 was interesting. She had twelve great grandchildren visit her for lunch. Mine were not there because we were out in Texas. She lived at that time with her bachelor son, Orlie. Around midnight, he heard her stirring around in her room so he got up to go see about her. She was putting on her Sunday clothes, including her gloves and hat. "Where do you think you're going, Mother?" Orlie asked. "Heaven,"

Grandma Collier answered. "I am getting ready to die. Call the doctor. I wanted to look nice when he came." And she sat down in the rocking chair and died. One of the last things she said was, "I'm sorry Marjorie's children couldn't come to lunch."

And About Grandpas

Where there are Grandmas, there must be Grandpas, and they influenced my life, as well.

Grandpa Walter Asa Collier was my Dad's Dad. He was an old railroad man and worked for Erie, Southern Pacific, and the Santa Fe Railroads. Because of him, later when I worked on the Pecos Independent newspaper, I wrote several features about railroads in Texas and won two awards from the Texas Railroad Association. The awards were clocks because of the legend that the railroads always operated on time. Well, they may have, but the clocks didn't. They were always slow. Grandpa Collier was a laid-back and happy man. He lived much of his life in Hornell, New York, so I didn't see him very often. But I knew a lot of Grandpa stories. One was that during the fight for Prohibition, his wife, Ollie, went around the block with a petition to do away with the sale of alcohol. Grandpa went around the block the other way, advocating keeping things like they were.

I was present the summer of 1939 in Hornell on the fourth of July, their 50th wedding anniversary. The local newspaper came to do a story on them and asked Grandpa, "Did you ever consider divorce?" And he answered calmly, "No, but I thought about murder a couple of times." Grandpa lived to be well into his eighties, and on the last day of his life, was reported to have said, "Well, Ollie was right. Beer and cigarettes finally got me."

My other Grandpa, Edward H. Diehl, was my mother's Dad and as different from Grandpa Collier as he could be. Grandpa Diehl was born in New Oxford, Pennsylvania. He was a late and only child, having been born after his mother was forty years old and after his parents had been married over twenty years. He was definitely spoiled. He was also brilliant. What a volatile combination. He was sent to Susquehanna University in Selingsgrove, Pennsylvania, in 1898 for a college education, when college educations were rare. Previous to that, he had married Dillie Kate Hoover, of a family distantly related to the late President Hoover. She was only fifteen, and he was nineteen when they were married. But his mother, who was a Spangler, didn't think she was going to be around much longer, and she wanted that marriage.

Ed was thought to be a good catch so the Hoovers urged the early marriage, as well. The couple went off to his college days where her brother, Harvey Daniel Hoover, was already a student studying to be a Lutheran minister. H. D. Hoover went ahead to excel all of his life as a pastor; at one time, he was president of Carthage College, and later a professor at the Lutheran Seminary in Gettysburg and editor of "Light for Today", a devotional booklet for the Lutheran Church.

Great Uncle Harvey was also one of the early representatives to the World Council of Churches for one branch of the Lutherans. He definitely influenced my life. He sent me post cards from all over the country where he spoke. Later, when I told my mother I was considering going to work for the church, she said, "Nobody in our family ever worked for the church." It had the tone of, "Nobody in our family ever went to jail." But I answered, "Great Uncle Harvey did." And mother answered, "Well, and look where it led him. He even helped with the first Revised Standard Bible. Hmphh." Mother really thought that was a Communist effort.

But back to Grandpa Diehl. He had fun at college. He played in sports. He joined a fraternity. He read a lot of books. He bought a beautiful edition of Shakespeare with golden edged pages. It seems money was no object in those days. He and Dillie had two children while at Susquehanna: one was my mother, Beatrice, and the other was Harvey, named for Dillie's brother.

Grandpa did graduate, but he did not become a Lutheran minister. He had gotten interested in photography and took pictures of everything. One of my Mother's early miserable memories was having to stand still while he took her picture. He also took a picture of the flower-draped coffin of President McKinley being taken back to Washington, D. C., by train after his assassination. The train went through Selinsgrove.

He moved to Philadelphia, and his parents bought him a car. There were only about seven in the whole city in 1906. He took pictures for a living and worked all week on his car so that the family could get in it on Sunday and drive down the street to go to the church with people coming out of their houses to watch them go by.

About then, somebody gave him a folder about South Texas. The folder indicated that people from the North were going there to put in orchards such as in Florida and were making so much money that they didn't know what to do with it all. This appealed to Grandpa.

He put his car and his family on a boat going down the Ohio River to the Mississippi and on to the Gulf of Mexico. They finally disembarked in Galveston and started driving to South Texas. There were no roads, but only wagon trails and railroads. At one point, they rode along the track. There were no motels, and they slept in barns. Grandma took malaria, which she had off and on the rest of her life. They finally came to Harlingen, which was the focal point of the folder. Grandpa didn't like the lay of the land—said it was too low; so he walked down the tracks fourteen miles to Mercedes, where he eventually made his new home.

Being a good Pennsylvania Dutchman, he built the barn first. Right after he finished the barn, a flood came from the Rio Grande River, and it washed away the rest of the lumber for the house. They finally did get the house constructed. It was not elaborate. It had a living and dining room, kitchen, and two bedrooms. The outhouse was back of the barn. The yard was huge, and he purchased one of the first power lawn mowers. They had grass tennis courts and croquet courts. They joined the Presbyterian Church and held socials for the congregation on their vast lawn.

Grandpa built what was the first garage to repair automobiles in South Texas. All those days of tinkering with his car had paid off. People that had cars came from miles around. One was George Parr of San Diego, Texas, who later became the kingpin to elect Lyndon Johnson as a Texas senator in one of the most questionable elections in the history of the state.

When Grandma died young, Grandpa became a recluse. He gave the garage to his son and son-in-law. He literally retired in his early forties. He read constantly. I recall sitting in his lap while he smoked a pipe and read James Whitcomb Riley poems to me. He refused to pay his taxes on property back in New Oxford and lost it all.

He tinkered with radios and repaired them for a radio shop in town. They would bring them out and pick them up. He rarely went to town. He ate the noon meal with us and washed the dishes afterward.

Mother and Dad were running a car parts store. Grandpa was our baby-sitter. Only he didn't sit much. He turned us loose to play on the twelve acres around our house. It's amazing we didn't fall out of the willow trees or drown in the irrigation canal. In the evening on some days, he would walk with us on the levee which was put in by the town to keep it from being flooded again. He would tell stories on the way. We had to tell stories on the way back. That's where I learned to tell stories.

In the early 30s, Grandpa invented what later would have been a solar heating unit. He got angry and tore it up. He invented what could have been a television. He tore that up, as well. My Dad used to say, "He needs to work for somebody like DuPont, and every time he invents something, they ought to take it away from him."

But it kept him busy. He lived to be almost ninety. He never completed an invention. He went to town only twice over the years. He went once to pick out a radio for me when I turned fifteen. He made them take off the back so he could look at the inside. That radio lasted 55 years without a part being replaced. He went once to town to get me a teddy bear when I turned sixteen because I wanted one. I, too, was spoiled.

Grandpa and Dad ate lunch together every day and argued about everything. But I only ever saw them really angry one time when Grandpa told Dad how smart the Germans were and how dumb the Irish were. That argument was wild.

At those noon meals, we often all talked at once. I am guilty of interrupting other people when they are talking to this day.

Grandpa had built on the higher land when he moved to Mercedes. He said the other side of town was a swamp. As the town developed, the fancier homes were built in the so-called swamp. Grandpa refused to cross the bridge on the main canal, even to go to the cemetery. We always drove down the highway and way around. The night after he died, the Tenth Street bridge suddenly split and fell in the canal. I always thought his ghost axed it. We had to drive three miles around to bury him. But even after death, he didn't cross that bridge.

Both parts of my family came from east of the Mississippi. I've heard it said that if you're born east of the Mississippi, you talk about who you are and from where you came. If you're born west of the Mississippi, you talk about who you are and where you are going. I'm proud to be from the West.

But I heard that "who you are and where you came from" as I grew up. All four of my Great, Great Grandpas fought at Gettysburg. Great, Great, Greats fought in the War of 1812 and the Revolution. There were names in the family, like Collier and Holmes and Diehl and Hoover, Spangler, Gable, and Downs, and tales about them all.

My favorite story was the Spangler distant cousin that was hanged after the Lincoln assassination. He was working backstage at the theater and held John Wilkes Booth's horse while he went inside. He was later proved to be innocent, but by then, he was very dead. I always related to that relative. I thought: there you would be, trying to do somebody a favor and hold his horse, and they come running to you and hang you to a tree. What a rotten break! But the Spangler family, in all of their glory, simply said, "Well, he shouldn't have gone to work at the theater; he should have stayed on the farm."

I always figured that as I ventured forth in my life that if anything happened to me, the family would simply have said, "Well, she should have stayed home."

Everybody Needs One

Everybody needs a family friend that is an odd-ball and that will help teach you to be an odd-ball. And I had one.

In Mercedes, there was a town character named Pres Allen. His wife had died, and he had returned to live at the home of his mother who was just over one hundred years old. Working in that household was a wonderful African American couple whose family had always worked for the Allens before the Civil War, during the Civil War, and after the Civil War. Their ancestors had helped hide the silver in the well in Georgia when Sherman was coming.

Pres had run a silver mine in Oklahoma and worked for the Cotton Exchange in New Orleans. He was interesting. He collected precious gems: rubies, diamonds, and also pieces of amber and moss agate that were not as precious, but equally as beautiful.

He loved horse races. He did not go to church. He wrote bad poetry. He loved the outdoors and natural beauty. He had opinions on every subject. He had traveled around the world—even to China. He said he believed in reincarnation which I had never heard about.

He read everything. He played cards and dominoes. He could quote the Bible. He became a friend of my father because he thought Dad was an extremely funny Irishman.

One night during each week and each Sunday afternoon, his chauffeur drove him to our house and let him out. Dad always took him home. He always stayed for supper. He brought foods I had never eaten because it was the Depression years, and they cost too much. He brought avocados and strawberry preserves. He brought a whole set of China dishes because his soup bowl had a crack in it.

The first time he came he said he was going to take home all the strawberry jam we didn't eat, and I tried to eat it all. I nearly got sick in the process. He always gave my brother and me one nickel each and told us to "spend it foolishly."

Later, he used to make ten cent bets with me on college football games. He told me he would give me $10 if I ever saw a dead, white mule. We traveled a lot in the Valley and went to the beach on picnics and went on rock hunts in the low-lying hills near Rio Grande City. I kept looking for a dead, white mule.

He brought me miniature animals from all over the world, made out of ivory, ebony, porcelain, and brass. Then he bought me a what-not stand on which to keep them. Then, he fussed at me if I didn't keep it dusted. He bought my mother a floor lamp for Christmas and got a big kick out of delivering it and telling me to hide it for a week. I hid it in my closet and threatened her if she opened the closet before Christmas.

He bought the lamp because he played bridge and hearts with them and had a hard time seeing the cards. When I was a senior in high school, he saw me looking at an expensive dress in the window of Mildred's expensive dress shop. He told me he would buy it for me if I would read, "The Decline of the West", by Spangler and report on it to him. It sounded like a western to me, so I agreed. It was a heavy book. It was not a western. It was about what was to happen years later; oil came into the Middle East, and the East became more powerful. By the time that happened, I knew all about it because of Pres Allen.

On his mother's 100th birthday, he bought her an elevator. The other two sons came to the party and many of the grandchildren. One of them was an associate editor at Time magazine. Mrs. Allen looked at him and asked, "Do you still work for that socialistic Time magazine?" He admitted that he did. She responded, "Then get the h—out of my house." And he did.

Like I say, they were characters. And I loved Pres like an extra Grandpa. One evening we were driving back from the beach and suddenly Pres screamed out, "Walter, Walter, pull over and stop the car." Dad stopped. Then Pres said, "That is the most beautiful sunset I have ever seen. Let's all get out and look at it."

Eventually, I saw a dead, white mule. We got out and looked at that, as well. And yes, I got the $10.

He gave me wonderful presents—a diamond ring, a moss agate bracelet, a cameo, a suitcase. He made me want to travel. He made me read. He later gave my daughters dolls that walked and an electric stove that really cooked.

He asked to be cremated and his ashes taken up in a plane and scattered over a place he loved—Mexico. So, it was done.

Everybody should be lucky enough to have a Pres Allen in their life. And if I'm an oddball, or an old curmudgeon at times, or a "mean old woman with a mission", part of the blame goes to Pres.

About Storms, Bananas, and Red Bicycles

Childhood is not always interesting, but some of the stories from mine are funny.

Even the worst hurricane the Valley ever had in South Texas in 1933 caused a story in my life. It rained and blew all night. I was seven years old and slept through it. Mother and Dad and my brother taped up all the windows to keep out the rain. It came in anyway. Dad tried to wake me up to help, but I slept on. He pulled the bed away from the window in case the glass broke. And I slept on. They rolled up the wool carpet and put it on the dining room table which was propped up with bricks because there was water all over the floor. And I slept on. They propped up the piano, as well. And I slept on. When morning came, I got up and put my feet into water and wondered what it was doing there, and I wanted breakfast. Never mind what they said. My Dad rarely used bad language, but he did that day. The lull from the storm came, and Dad walked a mile into town to see about his garage. He came back discouraged because the roof had blown off. About then, the storm hit again from the other direction. It blew and rained some more.

I wanted to bring in the hutch of pet rabbits that was outside. But Dad had a lot to say about that, as well. Something like, "the h—with the rabbits!" The hutch took off into the air. The rabbits were against the wire with their ears laid back, and they were flying. Peter Rabbit fell out. And he stayed in our yard for three years after that. We never penned him back up, but simply put apple peelings and potato peelings and lettuce by the back step for him. He learned to fight the dogs and cats by backing up and kicking them. He was one tough rabbit, and we loved him dearly. He would hop over and let us pet him. He survived that storm.

That same year when I was seven, Mother decided to give me a birthday party. It was the Depression years so you didn't have a party every year. But she said we could invite six little girls and "Marjorie makes seven to celebrate her seventh." Walter was sent away to go fishing with Harold Rippert. There were to be no boys present. But I told my friend Andrew about it when I was walking home from school, and he thought he was invited. So, as the party began, Andrew arrived all dressed up and carrying a present. Mother nearly had a fit. She called me aside and said that Andrew would get my favor because there were no extras. That was all right.

We began to play games. Mother said that in London Bridge, I, as birthday girl, and Nancy Prothro would be the bridge. Nancy was the daughter of one of Mother's friends. She was no friend of mine. She was two years older than me, and at that age, that's a big difference. I'd always played London Bridge when one was an apple and one was a banana. That worked out fine. I got to choose first and chose banana. Nancy said she was going to be a silver princess in a golden chariot. I said, "No, you have to be an apple." She said, "No, you don't know much. I can be anything I want to . . ." I tried to change to something better, but she said, "No, you've already chosen. YOU are a banana."

So be it. The little girls went through the bridge one by one and needless to say, nobody picked banana; they all ended up behind Nancy Prothro. Then, along came Andrew, and he staunchly chose "Banana." In those days, we drew a line and tried to pull the other side across. Andrew and I pulled so hard that he tore my yellow organdy dress, but we dragged those six little girls across the line. We won, even if I was a banana.

Years later, when speaking a the Presbyterian Outlook breakfast in Cincinnati when I was running for moderator of the Presbyterian General Assembly being held there, I used that same story. I said, "I'm not a learned theologian. But I know that even a banana can win, and I do love this church, and love mission, and love the Lord." Well, this banana won.

My friends, Joy Henning and Carol Adcock went out and bought bananas to put in the moderator's suite after I won. They didn't place them in a bowl. They put them on the counter and on the coffee table and on the dining table and on the piano and on my pillow and one in the bathtub and one on the commode seat. The banana had won.

Mother made one other attempt at a birthday party a few years later. My brother's birthday was two weeks after mine so she had a combined wiener roast on a Friday night to celebrate both birthdays. One of the boys was Catholic and couldn't eat a hotdog on Friday. I'd never heard of a Catholic. All of us kids were Presbyterian, Methodist, Baptist, or Lutheran. I had certainly never known anybody that couldn't eat a hotdog. I thought it was the strangest thing I had ever heard. But Mother simply went inside and fixed a tuna fish sandwich and told me she would explain later. And she did. I still don't understand it.

Now, what's this about red bicycles? My parents did not allow me to have a bicycle, thinking it was too dangerous. And they may have been right since one time I went through a barbed wire fence riding Jean Sproles' bicycle, probably because I had never been allowed to ride one.

But in the third grade, a boy named Mack George came to school on a new, shiny, red bicycle. Now, Mack lived next door to our church in a two-story house—a big house. His father was some kind of engineer, and he lived in exciting places like South America. On Valentine's Day, he gave me a beautiful Valentine. It has a special seal and under the seal was a quarter. That was a lot of money during the Depression. I was impressed. Not only that, he let me ride home on the back of his new red bicycle. I was overwhelmed. I was in love. But as luck would have it, the engineer got sent far away to some foreign land, and Mack and the red bicycle went along. I always did have bad luck with my love life. I wonder what ever happened to Mack George.

About Cheese Sandwiches

Back in 1936, Dad, my brother, Walter, and I had made our first trip across Texas. I had been raised in the Lower Rio Grande Valley, that lush area along the Texas-Mexican border where oranges and Ruby Red grapefruit grew, where the tall palm trees waved in the breeze, and where you could go across the river to Mexico or across the bay to Padre Island for a taste of the sea breeze.

We went to Padre Island at least twice a year. Mother approved of that. But we never crossed the Rio Grande to the neighboring country of Mexico because Mother still held the fear built in by the years when those living on the border hid their guns under the bed because "Pancho Villa" was coming.

Dad had run away from home and joined the Cavalry when he was seventeen to fight Pancho Villa, and that's how he ended up in Texas. But that's another tale.

The towns in the Valley nearly touch each other. It's seven miles from Harlingen to La Feria, five to Mercedes, six to Weslaco, and eight to Donna; then, you come to Alamo, San Juan, and Pharr whose city limits are across the street from each other. Then, Pharr runs right into McAllen.

I thought the whole world was like that and when we started off across the great King Ranch to Falfurrias that summer I was ten years old, I thought we were coming to the dropping-off place. I began to fret and ask where the next town might be. My father's laughter was no comfort. I looked gloomily out at the mesquite bushes and cactus as we passed. I fell asleep. When I awoke, the scenery had not changed. I went back to sleep and waking the second time, I saw we were coming into the edges of San Antonio. I looked in amazement. Here was still another world.

It seemed to hold a lot of the Mexican people that were prevalent down home, but it was crowded and hurried and different. I tried to be happy about it, but in 1936 in the Texas summer heat, I was more hot than happy. I also was hungry. I began to whine. We stopped for lunch. I had eaten out only once before—maybe twice. You couldn't afford to eat out in the Depression. I even carried a sack lunch to school, instead of spending a quarter at the cafeteria. So I scanned the restaurant menu, hunting something familiar—anything. "Cheese sandwich," I stated firmly. "I want a cheese sandwich." But I didn't get off that easy. "No, you don't," Dad said and added, "I promised your mother you would eat right." He ordered the plate lunch for all of us, with veal cutlets. I had never even heard of veal cutlets, but I instantly knew that I would hate them. When they came, the looks of them did nothing to alleviate my fear. I stared at the plate. I took a bite. "Ughh," I muttered. "Eat your lunch," Dad stressed and added, "Walter is eating his." Good for Walter. I ate another bite. I pushed the food around on my plate. Dad had finished. Walter had finished. Dad glared and said, "Eat." By then, I had absolutely had it. We had left home on a fun trip. I had never been that far from home. The scenery was boring. The car was hot. The food was gross. I missed my mother. Big tears welled up and began to fall on my plate. The waitress at the High Hat Café gave my father a stern look. Dad tired of the problem. "Let's go," he said, "And for all I care, you can eat cheese sandwiches the rest of the trip. Let's go see the Alamo."

And I did eat cheese sandwiches the rest of the trip. I became an expert on cheese sandwiches across Texas and New Mexico. And the best ones were at the Nimitz Hotel in Fredricksburg. That's the family hotel of Admiral Nimitz, who became famous later. They had homemade bread and homemade cheese. Definitely the best.

Speaking of the Famous

Talking about Nimitz, who later became famous, makes me think about people who are considered famous.

I've had the opportunity to meet so many of them. Most of them came across to me as just wonderful people who had to put up with their fame. A few of them came across to me as arrogant, but there is no telling how I was coming across to them.

I have met and interviewed every President since Truman, except Nixon, and I interviewed Spiro Agnew, his vice president.

I got to talk to Eleanor Roosevelt when I was in junior high attending Rotary International Lectures with my father in Harlingen, Texas. I interviewed General Eisenhower in San Antonio, Jack Kennedy in Washington, D. C., Lyndon Johnson in Kingsville, Texas, Gerald Ford in Big Spring, Texas, Jimmy Carter in Atlanta, Ronald Reagan in Odessa, Texas, George Bush in Pecos, Texas, and other places, and Bill Clinton in Little Rock.

Besides Agnew, I interviewed and talked to Cactus Jack Garner at his 95th birthday party which was attended by LBJ, Truman, and Sam Rayburn, among others.

Other candidates interviewed included Barry Goldwater in Odessa, Bob Dole in Lubbock, Lloyd Bentsen in Big Spring, Gary Hart in Atlanta, Walter Mondale in Chevy Chase, Jesse Jackson in Atlanta, and others.

Ford came across to me as the most real. He didn't always know where he was and discussed Colorado sugar beets while in Oklahoma. He tried to eat the shucks on the tamales in San Antonio because he didn't know what they were.

Both Johnson and Clinton came across to me as arrogant. Although many would disagree. I was very young the first time I met Johnson. He was running for Senator against Coke Stevenson, and I was a teacher when he came to a reception in Kingsville. That was the race where many claim that Johnson only won three days after the election was over and by less than 100 votes, including a list of alphabetically-lined-up dead people in San Diego, Texas.

I was in my first year of teaching—just out of Texas A & I. Johnson told us how he was going to get us all federal aid for education. I argued with him around the punch bowl, maintaining that I didn't want federal aid for education. Of course, I didn't have to balance the school budget. I told him I would never vote for him, and I never did.

Later, I almost reconsidered when he was running for President in 1964, because of Lady Bird. I liked her.

A lot of the women reporters in Texas were invited to the Johnson Ranch by Lady Bird. The only paper in the state that had come out against Johnson was our Pecos Independent. So, I was not invited. But my friend, Sarah McClendon, in Washington called up Liz Carpenter and asked if I was overlooked because we had exposed Estes. A lot of ties between Estes and LBJ were considered apparent by many. So, to avoid that confrontation, I received a late telegram inviting me to the ranch.

I rode by bus to the event. Lady Bird was such a class act that I almost reconsidered my vote. But I decided she wasn't the one for whom I would be voting.

That barbecue was wonderful. Some of the cabinet wives were there, including Nellie Connelly, Mrs. Humphrey, and two or three others. We were given books, straw hats, and all kinds of things. We had a glorious time. If it had been Lady Bird running, I'd have voted for her in a minute.

I also was lucky enough to go on one of Lady Bird's famous raft trips. In 1966, I heard that she was taking a trip on the Rio Grande, but I paid little attention. I was then news editor of the Andrews County News in West Texas and knew that no small paper would be invited. My publisher, James Roberts, stopped at my desk one morning and said rather snidely, "Well, you say you know Liz Carpenter. Why don't you get invited on the Lady Bird raft trip?"

I decided to try and wrote her a letter. The next week, James' sister, Louise, ran up to my desk rather excited and said, "Marj, they say the White House is on the phone and wants to talk to you." I tried to act nonchalant, but the long and short of it was that I did get to go. I had a little problem. I rarely ever get colds, but I had a terrible one that turned into what my doctor called "walking pneumonia". I was determined to go anyway—and go I did. It was a fantastic experience. We went to Marfa and welcomed the First Lady's plane, and then we went on to the Big Bend National Park.

My roommate at the Chisos Mountain Lodge was to be Barbara Funkenhouser from the El Paso Times. Boy, we were treated royally! I remember there were special cards welcoming us and flowers and whiskey and cartons of cigarettes, baskets of fruit, and a small travel case for each. Incredible! Barbara didn't come so I had it all.

The reporters from the larger publications may have been use to such treatment, but I was shocked.

Stuart Udall, Secretary of the Interior, was along on the trip and later we were given special certificates calling us "Raft Riders of the Rio Grande".

On the first night we walked up the mountain to watch Lady Bird plant a tree and then on up to a campfire and a "hoax lecture" by Cactus Jack Pryor, who ran one of Lady Bird's radio stations in Austin. He played an old prospector that night.

I later saw him play a Russian spy. He was really talented. Back in Andrews, my eleven year old son, Jim Bob, stayed at the home of Kenneth Bales, who had three sons. They were all out in the front yard playing football when Jim Bob suddenly looked at his watch and came running in the house. He turned on the television and sat down. "What are you doing?" Kenneth asked. "I want to watch the six o'clock news and see if Mama got to where Lady Bird is," Jim Bob stated. Kenneth explained, "They won't show your mama. Go on back out and play until supper time." Jim Bob answered, "They always show Mama when she goes places. I'll wait." Kenneth recalled, "The news showed Lady Bird and Udall planting a tree and then walking up the hill. Suddenly, they showed Marj sitting on a rock, halfway up the hill, and Jim Bob said, "There she is. She got there." And he went back out to play."

That whole trip was incredible. We dedicated the improvements at Fort Davis. The Pecos band played, and my daughter, Cathy, was a twirler, and my daughter, Carolyn, played the French horn.

We rode rafts down the river and had boxes of fried chicken for lunch on a sandbar. That night, we had a barbecue and open bar with the Ector County Sheriff's Posse providing the food. That's the way to go camping—go with Lady Bird.

On my raft was Andrew Brown from National Geographic, a reporter from Houston, a park ranger, and me. We nearly sank at one point, and I saved the Geographic camera from going under water. I corresponded with Andrew for years after that incident.

Sometimes It Was Funny

There was one funny incident on the Lady Bird raft trip worth reporting. Those reporters with cameras were taken ahead and let out on a sandbar so that we could get good pictures of Lady Bird coming down the river. We all set up cameras.

One eager, young reporter from a West Texas newspaper waded to the other side of the river and climbed the bank. This put him in the background of everybody else's pictures. The photographer from Life magazine took a dim view of this. He hollered for him to get down off the bank. The lad stood. Then, the photographers began to chunk rocks and clods at him. He slid down to the river and came back across. Whereupon the Life photographer said, "Reporters are strange. Sometimes we go for a scoop or a different angle, but there are occasions that we're just like bananas and hang in a bunch. This, son, is a banana day."

Gerald Ford came to Big Spring in support of Bill Fisher, the GOP candidate for Congress. It didn't help him because the Democrat, Charles Stenholm, wiped him out.

Ford went on to Abilene where he celebrated his birthday. I got a piece of that five foot tall cake. When they were preparing for the barbecue for Ford in Big Spring, the assistant principal, Craig Fischer, called from the high school and asked for the names of some of my church youth group boys to help set the tables. I gave him the names of Bill Little, Derek Horton, Kent Ivey, Doug Mays, and several others. They were excused from school to go out and get things ready. They were putting white butcher paper on the tables, instead of cloth, and had no way to cut it from the roll. One of the youths, Kent Ivey, pulled out a huge knife and cut the paper. The Secret Service went crazy. They came running over and told Kent, "We'll hold that weapon for you until the barbecue is over." Said Kent, "Well, at least let us cut the paper first."

One time I attended Barry Goldwater's wedding anniversary. It was a party in Odessa when he was campaigning. Reporters were not welcome, but the ones traveling with him were invited and asked to keep the party a personal thing and not report it as a news event. Sarah McClendon got me invited. An Odessa reporter came into the party uninvited and began to take notes; he was picked up by the elbows and thrown out the door.

The national reporters pooled donations and presented the Goldwaters a beautiful Native American urn. Goldwater said, "Since I already know that some of you disagree with me to the point that you want to throw up, I doubly appreciate the thoughtful gift." He then presented his wife with a charm of balloons for her charm bracelet. The balloons were to remind her of his nomination at the GOP convention which had a hall filled with balloons.

I remember when I met Clinton at a cocktail party at the Governor's mansion in Little Rock when he was governor. He gave the party for the officers of the National Federation of Press Women, and I was one of the officers. You could tell that he was obviously running for something, although none of us dreamed it was to be President.

I remember going to a party in D.C. the week that George Bush was inaugurated as President. The party was small for a Presidential week celebration, and nobody from out of town was to be invited. But Sarah insisted that I go with her. I was standing back in a corner, eating my chips and guacamole and trying to keep from being noticed. Sam Donaldson came over and said, "You're not from here. Who are you?" I answered, because I was miffed, "I'm Marj Carpenter; who are you?" (Of course, I really knew.) He looked angry and said, "How did you get to this party?" And I answered, "I came with Sarah." Since Sarah had been a reporter in Washington longer than any of them, that was a good answer. Sam grinned and shrugged his shoulders and said, "Oh, well." I kind of crept out of my corner and visited with folks and had a wonderful conversation with Justice Sandra Day O'Conner.

I met Reagan when he was running for the nomination for President four years before he was nominated. He made a swing into West Texas and was to appear at the Midland/Odessa Airport and Permian Basin College in Odessa. I was hoping to cover that event, but my editor was in a snit with me about something and decided to send the newest cub reporter instead. That was Jamie Werrell, fresh out of Colgate University and trying to figure out West Texas.

I lived just across the street from the paper and had gone home for something. As I came back, Jamie was standing by his car and called me over. "They just told me to go to the airport and cover Reagan for President." "Are you cleared for Secret Service?" I asked. "No," he said. Then he added, "As a matter of fact, I don't even know the way to the Midland Airport." "Oh, for heaven's sake," I said, "Those idiots." Then I added, "Get in the car," and I got in the other side. "They'll have a fit," Jamie said. "I heard them say they weren't going to let you cover this one." "They'll never figure out where I am," I said. "Drive, or you're not going to get there in time."

Sure enough, as we pulled into the Midland Airport, the entourage with Reagan was already leaving. "Get in the parade," I said. Jamie was driving a very dirty Peugeot. We got in behind a lot of limos and big Cadillacs. As we rounded the curve headed for the college, there was a highway patrolman in the road. "Oh, oh," Jamie said. I leaned forward, "Hi, Buff," and away we went. I covered wrecks and knew all the patrolmen in the area. As we neared a gate, we could see additional guards. I told Jamie, "Don't look at him. Look straight ahead. Look important and keep blinking your headlights. We blinked on through. As we were getting out, Jamie said, "Now, how do we get inside?" "That's a good question," I said. "You have no credentials," and again added, "Those idiots!"

Then, I saw Judge Barbara Culver. She was the Republican judge of Midland County, and I often attended meetings that she was attending. She hollered, "Marj, come meet Reagan." I grabbed Jamie's elbow and dragged him on over. We talked to Barbara and to Ronald Reagan and followed them right on into the hall with no credentials at all.

I went way over in the corner and leaned against the wall, staying away from the TV cameras. I didn't want to get fired. One young woman from Odessa, Pat Pearson, asked me, "Why are you hanging back? It's not like you." "Because I am not here," I answered.

We drove back to Big Spring, and Jamie wrote his story. I heard one of the editors say to the other, "The new reporter did a good job. I don't know how he got in, but even Marj might not have pulled that off." I bit my lip and said nothing. However, Jamie, when he later became editorial page editor in Rockhill, South Carolina, wrote a column about the incident when I was in town there as moderator of the Presbyterian

General Assembly of the church. He said, "She may be the big pooh-bah for the Presbyterians, but to me, she's the reporter that got me in to cover Ronald Reagan."

I covered Governor Wallace at the airport that year, as well. That was right when they were attempting to close Webb Air Force Base in Big Spring, and my question to Wallace was on that subject. He also was running for a Presidential nomination.

That day, my son at the University of Texas had come home from work and turned on the six o'clock news. Wallace came on, and he said, "Oh, no," and asked his roommate to switch channels. But then, he suddenly hollered, "Don't touch that dial. There's Mama!"

And there Mama was, and as was often the case—putting her foot in the durn petunias.

Who Else Is Famous?

Who decides who is really famous? Reporters get to cover all kinds of folks—entertainers, athletes, politicians, successful business people, leading professors and theologians, military leaders, and others.

I don't know where to start and stop so I'll just reach for memories...

Vic Damone singing "Red Roses for a Blue Lady" and walking across the floor of a night club to present me a red rose.

Michael Langdon turning his horse in the middle of the rodeo arena in Big Spring where he was the star attraction and trotting up to the box where I sat and saying, "Hon, thanks for the interview and the kind words."

Country singer Johnny Rodriquez telling me about going to jail for stealing a goat.

John Wayne at a coffee shop in Pecos, "I'm on the way through to get down to Brackettville to film a scene for a movie."

Peter Greaves and I who literally ran into each other going in two different directions at the opening of the Ramada Inn in Pecos. He fell fully clothed into the swimming pool, delaying the ribbon cutting.

Hank Williams, Jr., who was fascinated that I had actually heard Hank Williams, Sr. in Louisiana.

Senator John Tower as he refused to shake hands with Bob Krueger who had allegedly said some damaging things about Tower.

Bob Lilley, a Dallas Cowboy football player, who was in town for the official opening of the Coors Warehouse.

Robert Mitchum, three sheets in the wind, at a party after a horse race in Ruidosa, insisting that I was older than he was. He couldn't believe I'd watched his movies as a teenager.

Al and Bobby Unser when they were working at the Tire Test Track outside Pecos "at the only place we can practice driving fast legally."

Lloyd Bentsen sitting by my desk at the Big Spring Herald as I wrote a story about his campaign.

Dan Reeves, later the Atlanta Falcon football coach, interviewed in Andrews as he spoke at the Sports Banquet.

Quail Dobbs, best know rodeo clown who saved many a bull rider from injury, as he stood talking to Toots Mansfield, one of the world's best ropers ever.

Bishop Desmond Tutu who said, "The White man came to South Africa, and we had the land and they had the Bible." He said, "Let's pray." We shut our eyes, and now they have the land and we have the Bible."

Ginger Rogers, who when I asked whether she'd rather dance or act, did a quick dance step or two and said, "Does that answer your question?"

Liz Taylor, who hosted a barbecue on the John Warner farm in Virginia, and Barbara Bush called me over and introduced me. Liz was pretty and also pretty full of herself.

Helen Walton of Wal-Mart, who has been so important to the Presbyterian church. I'll never tell where we had the most fun.

Allen Boesak, who as he struggled with the anti-apartheid movement, gained fame, but got his personal life into a shambles; however, he is still one of the world's great preachers.

Peter Jennings, Tom Brokaw, Dan Rather, Larry King, Judy Woodruff, and all the others I met as I helped returning hostage Ben Weir with his publicity.

Ben Weir, himself—gentle Ben—who never realized he was famous.

Charles Kirbo, who was one of Jimmy Carter's advisors, saying at lunch at an Atlanta bank, "Being at the top of the government or the top of a church is both rewarding and frustrating."

John Fife, whose fame during the Salvadorian refugee news was something he was very shy about.

Charlie Johnson, once the Denver Bronco quarterback who always had a good time when he came home to Big Spring and sang around Julie Shirey's piano.

Ralph Yarbrough accepting a huge $50,000 check at a Billie Sol Estes barbecue, having his picture made receiving it, and later forgetting that he had ever received it.

Tom Gillespie, Randy Taylor, James Costen, John Mulder, Hartley Hall, Doug Oldenburg, Heath Rada, Arlo Duba, and David Ramadge—all Presbyterian seminary presidents as they traveled together to seminaries in eastern Europe as the Iron Curtain shattered, and the Berlin Wall went down.

And Jack Stotts and Sam Callian, the other seminary presidents, who did not make that trip but appeared often around the church.

Mister Roberts as he worked with the children at the Presbyterian Peacemaking event on Long Island.

Gary Hart as he tried to break up the Atlanta Press Club's Christmas party for a press conference. I told him, "Gary, you don't have sense enough to be President, if you try to break up a Christmas party."

All of the wonderful CNN folks that I met each year at the annual Gary Rowe party in January.

Red Adair, the oil well fire fighter, as he explained how he got into such a business, and then would jump aside slightly when a light flickered.

Andy Eddington, who talked to a young Adolph Hitler on the docks in Germany.

DeWitt Reddick, who taught journalism at the University of Texas and had such pupils as Lady Bird, Nellie Connelly, and Walter Cronkite, just to name a few.

Tammy Wynette singing "Stand by Your Man" for a congressional candidate who lost in Abilene, Texas.

Charles Stenholm, the Congressional candidate who won and went on to win for many years and was often in the news.

Diane Sawyer, being installed in the Atlanta Press Club and Sarah McClendon and Helen Thomas, speaking to the National Federation of Press Women.

Bob Wills and his Texas Playboys, whom my husband and I drove two hundred miles to hear.

The Platters as they prepared to sing in an ecumenical communications gathering in Nashville, and I got to help serve them lunch.

Dick Van Dyke at an event in Atlanta, talking backstage to the widow of the doctor who delivered his first child.

Steve Allen as he tried to help the Presbyterian Pittsburgh media preparing spots to help bring home Ben Weir.

Roy Rogers and Dale Evans as they came out of a church service at Apple Valley Presbyterian Church.

Evel Knievel at an overnight stop at a Big Spring motel when he was driving out west for a jump.

This is endless—there are many more, but it's starting to get boring. I don't like name-dropping, but I wanted to show what a wonderful variety you meet as a reporter. Who's really famous anyway? Who isn't? I enjoyed meeting them all.

The Chapter That I Hate

This is one story of my life that I do not even like to recall, but I don't think I can completely ignore it. It is the story of the death of my husband, C.T. (Tex) Carpenter, Jr., in May, 1965.

He was very blue and discouraged about the continuous conflict in Pecos which often festered between the newspaper where I worked and the bank where he used to work.

He also was moody to start with after World War II. He had fought on D Day and was on the Susan B. Anthony—the only ship sunk. They were put on landing boats without their weapons in the hurry to get off the ship. So they had to use weapons found on dead soldiers—on either side.

He also fought at Hertgon Forest and told of the man in the foxhole with him being killed by shrapnel. He had to stay in that position all night with his dead friend. He had terrible nightmares every year when the weather first turned cold.

He told of being "one of two fools who said they could swim" and who swam out to take the cables under fire to re-bridge the Rhine. He earned a Purple Heart while crossing Europe with the combat engineers and was one of the first American groups into Berlin.

To make a long story short, I came home one Friday night from the junior high band concert, having gone to two parties to take pictures for the newspaper, and having delivered my oldest child to spend the night with a friend. The other two and I came home to find Tex dead on the den floor from a shotgun wound. It was ruled accidental death, but we were never sure.

I do remember that the community wrapped their arms around us and came and brought every kind of flower and food and prayer and consolation that they could think of at the time. I have one funny memory of Waddles, the dog. That dog had gotten in the habit of following Carolyn and her friend Johnny Toone up the ladder into the tree house. After they outgrew the tree house, the dog went up by himself and looked around. He was a bird dog that thought he was a bird.

In all of the excitement and confusion after my husband's death, somebody left the back gate open and Waddles ran up the street with the Rev. Jack Ware flapping along behind him and successfully collaring the dog.

When it was all over and the school year had ended, I got word that my Dad had a stroke. So we took off for Mercedes to see about him and my mother. He was a little improved and home with a walker. They didn't have a telephone because Mother didn't like phones. So the police came out to the house to tell me I had an emergency call.

The children and I rode into the telephone office to place a call. The children said, "What could it be?" I said, "I've been expecting the newspaper to fold up, and my job will be gone. Or maybe the house burned down. Pray that it's just the job."

That's what it was, but fortunately James Roberts over in Andrews, Texas, also had called and offered me another job as soon as I could take it.

I went back to the car to tell the kids what had happened. They were glad I had another job, but the girls set up a howl about moving to Andrews. They were getting ready to be a sophomore and senior in Pecos.

Through a lot of manipulating and getting friends and neighbors to help, my son and I moved to Andrews and the girls stayed in Pecos and finished high school. They proved children didn't need parents. They both were Best-All-Around, band sweetheart and drum major, DAR Good Citizen and all kinds of awards. Cathy was salutatorian, and Carolyn was fourth in her class.

I wore out two cars and many tires driving back and forth 100 miles every weekend and sometimes in between, if an emergency came about. I also kept my Presbyterian youth group on Sunday night in Pecos, and I helped with a teenage club in Andrews so I was working with young people in both towns. It was not an easy time. Jim Bob and I got up at 5 A.M. on Mondays, and he rode 97 miles to school, stopping in Kermit for breakfast.

I remember that when I made my very first trip to move to Andrews and Jim Bob and I drove off with the car full of clothes and stuff, I was crying most of the way. My son was huddled up very quietly in the back seat. Right before we got into Andrews, he leaned forward and said, "I just thought of something good." For a nine-year old leaving his home and sisters and going to a new place, I wondered what it could be . . . and asked.

I'll never forget his answer, and I laughed all the way into Andrews.

"We're not taking the piano with us," he stated, "so I don't have to take any more piano lessons."

Third Section

Some Petunia Beds I've Stepped Into

Contents

At the Old Oregon Mission 91

Inside Cuba 93

More About Cuba 96

Don't Go to Junkanoo 100

Celebrating an Inauguration 104

Into the Water I Went 107

A Day to Remember 109

The Rat and I 112

They Tell You Where to Go 114

And The Embassy Was Closed 117

About Visiting Jails 120

George Bush's Big Day 123

About Covering Plane Crashes 125

And Military Airplane Crashes 127

Stories That I Can't Forget 129

Where is Cochabamba and Where is Marj? 131

Favorite Reporters 133

Is This a New Chinese Word? 136

The Piano and I 138

The Computer and I 141

The Airplane and I 143

Yes, She Was There 146

What Keeps You Going 148

Writing About the Old West 150

With My Back to the Wall 152

So Slow Down, Marj–Who Sez? 154

The Best Days of my Life 156

And the Very Best 159

At the Old Oregon Mission

In the 1800s, two Presbyterian couples, Dr. Marcus and Narcissa Whitman and the Rev. Henry and Eliza Spalding went overland to Old Oregon and actually opened the Oregon Trail. They were sponsored by the Ithaca, New York, Presbyterian Church since the national office seemed to want no part of it.

The women in the group rode mules sidesaddle most of the way. They established a mission for the Indians (and in those days, they called them Indians).

The Whitmans settled among the Cayuse near what is now Lewiston, Idaho. The Spaldings were near Walla Walla, Washington. Both couples labored to build their homes, establish schools, start worship services, care for the sick, teach basic agriculture, and support themselves in farming.

The mission lasted eleven years. Tension increased because earlier settlers going out for gold seemed to be taking over the land. They also brought measles, a fatal disease to the Indians. The fact that whites didn't die of measles while the Indians did seemed to point to them that they were being poisoned by Dr. Whitman. This tragically climaxed when Cayuse leaders killed the Whitmans, some of their adopted children, and a number of the settlers, who were temporarily at Wailatpu, the place of the rye grass.

Miraculously, an enduring church was established among the Nez Perce.

One hundred years later, the Presbyterians were holding a memorial service for the "massacre" at Walla Walla. I went out to cover it for the news office of the church.

And that's when I got my foot into it. I saw my Native American friends on the back pew and sat down in the middle of them, chatting over happenings in the church. Midway in the service, the Native Americans sitting all around me suddenly stood and objected to the anniversary being called a massacre. They went on to explain the history from their point of view and how many of the Indians had their men and horses forced off into the Columbia Gorge where they died in the fall after this particular incident. There I sat right in the middle of them and everybody turned and glared, especially at me. But the long and short of it was that they talked to each other and set a second meeting to be held at Warm Springs Indian Reservation where they hoped reconciliation would take place. An offering there went to help prepare Native American young people as pastors.

A good time to have my foot into it. I persuaded the Portland newspaper to go down and cover that second meeting and give them some publicity. Later when the Native American council from the former northern-based church disbanded, they presented me with a pottery tile on a leather strap that depicted a jackrabbit. And they said, "Because you hop around the church and cover news for all of us."

Inside Cuba

It's difficult to go to Cuba with the boycott. It seems to be a little bit easier in recent years, but the first time I went in 1989, it was "major doings".

From the minute I stepped into the section of the Miami airport where charter planes left for Havana, I knew it was going to be a trip different from any I had ever taken.

The details of the trip were vague to me. This was because I had missed the original charter taken by the large group of members of the North American and Caribbean Council of the World Alliance of Reformed Churches. That was how we were going into the area.

The stated clerk of the Presbyterian Church, Jim Andrews and I had to attend the General Assembly Council meeting in Columbia, South Carolina, so we were two days late. Also late was the Rev. Margrethe Brown, presbyter of Genesee Presbytery in Rochester, New York. I didn't know Margrethe, but I knew Jim so I thought I would find him at the gate. He wasn't there, but there were dozens of Cubans there pushing forward to wait in line. It was a kind of orderly pushing. I watched with fascination.

They all had huge bundles they were taking to relatives in Cuba. I thought as I saw them all waiting, "Gee, the plane must be leaving soon." I had a moment of panic, but since it was four hours until the plane left, I needn't have worried.

I went back into the main portion of the airport hunting Andrews. I didn't have a ticket that was going to get me on that airplane. I had my passport and a Cuban visa. I had Andrews paged. Nobody came. I went back to the gate and back to the information desk and had him paged again. Margrethe turned up, but not Andrews. We went back to the gate. The man at the desk said, "Oh, you're part of the three from Atlanta—wait over there . . ." and he pointed to a wall. We joined two German gentlemen who were also "waiting over there."

Watching the Cuban-Americans push forward and weigh their luggage proved to be fascinating. They told one energetic young woman that her bag was fifteen pounds overweight. She jerked out of line, went behind a pole, unzipped the bag and took out cowboy boots, added two pairs of socks and put them on her feet. She tied a heavy jacket around her waist. She stuffed two pairs of blue jeans in her skirt. She took the bag back, and it was the correct weight. The fifteen pounds were now on her.

After another hour, Andrews arrived. We were the last three passengers on the plane. When Andrews was told that his bag couldn't go, he knelt down to take a change of clothes out of his suitcase. "Now you look like a Cuban," I told him. He didn't answer. He was carrying a box of medication to Cuba for a sick child. That later proved to be an interesting matter at the arriving airport in Cuba. Although it had taken a long time to get on the plane, the flight was "just the twink of an eye.'" In no time, Cubans were joyfully pointing out the lights of Havana. They still miss their homeland, and they care about their families there.

We quickly landed and for some reason, I went through customs with the greatest of ease. However, an official pointed to the exit and said, "Salida." He did not allow me to stay inside and wait for my two friends. So I was suddenly in Cuba, a little sooner than I had expected. I was the first one through customs. The guard outside with a gun on his hip said something in Spanish about getting me a taxi. He was wanting me off that sidewalk. I muttered something about "dos amigos" and he nodded. Just across the street, there were over 100 Cubans waiting for relatives to arrive. They were standing in a huge semi-circle, and some came up to ask me if I had seen their relatives and called them by name. Before I could answer in my pitiful Spanish, the guard became agitated and began to yell and wave his arms. He made quite a speech, and at one point pointed the gun up in the air and shot three times. Everybody pushed back further across the street. He spat out a few more phrases, and they moved back a little further. Some moved quickly. Some moved sullenly. Nobody left. Their relatives might come out of that door at any moment.

I waited and wondered. I leaned on the wall. I scanned the crowd. I didn't see anybody that looked Presbyterian to me. I wondered about my two traveling companions. Andrews was back at the customs desk, explaining about the medicine. They had sent for a doctor to examine it and see what it was.

Margrethe told me later that when they heard the shots outside, Andrews said, "I think Marj has gotten outside and started World War III." My foot was definitely back in the petunia patch, and I hadn't done a thing.

More About Cuba

After I got through customs upon my trip to Cuba, I stood quietly with my back against the wall, trying not to make a sound and hoping somebody would come. About then a pleasant-looking man asked the guard in Spanish if he had seen any Americanos. I caught that word anyway, and I said, "Are you hunting Jim Andrews? Are you Presbyterian?" "Yes," he answered, and I met the welcoming party. I was so glad to see those four Cuban Christians who had driven from Matanzas to go in and tell Andrews that they were waiting. Andrews' comment to me was, "How did you get outside?"

I went back outside and sat in the van and waited until they had cleared customs. We then drove into the night to Matanzas. Since I had been up since "before breakfast" in South Carolina, my vitality was beginning to flag. I nodded as we drove through the night. I remember stopping at a very small café where they seemed to sell rum, some kind of sandwiches, and small cups of stout coffee. I remember being grateful for the coffee and crawling back into the van.

At 3:30 in the morning, we arrived at the Evangelical Theological Seminary and Margrethe and I were assigned a room with two very gracious roommates, Una Matthews from Guyana and Jane Dempsey Douglas from Princeton who got up and turned on the light and helped us get settled.

From then on, I stayed confused the entire time that I was in Cuba. The Presbyterians there spoke of hope for growth and pride in survival. A missionary, Lois Kroehler, had been there since 1949, refusing to leave.

The Cubans were quick to tell you that they had gotten rid of the gambling and prostitution in Havana, which used to serve the tourist industry. These were all facts and commendable.

The children seen on the street did not seem to be as malnourished as children in many other developing countries. But, they had not shared the wealth; they had shared the poverty.

Everybody works for the government. Every job is under the government. They claim not to be burdened with shortages, but this is not true.

One morning I got up and went out and got my foot in the petunias again. I walked to the market which we had been told not to do. I was taking pictures of the long early morning line of people waiting to purchase meat. This upset them, and one woman ran at me and threatened to put me in jail. She reached for my camera, and I ran across the street. I had a picture in there I had taken the evening before from a high point on the seminary grounds looking down into the bay where there was a Russian submarine. I knew I was going to have to roll that picture out or expose all my pictures.

About then, thankfully, Tom Chavez, who was part of our group, came along and told them in Spanish that I was just "a silly old lady from the church." So they left me alone. Thank you, Tom.

I became very confused in that country. Although there has been no real effort at birth control such as in China, there are less children when the women are working and birth control is available. I thought of countries with poor children begging and countries where the concept is to have a lot of children so some will live to care for you in your old age. I couldn't pick a side in that debate.

To me, the lack of freedom in the country was so frustrating that it would absolutely paralyze the very fiber of my being.

What finished me off was a block meeting. They required us to attend. It seemed to serve an area of some ten or twelve blocks. We were invited there by the Committee to Defend the Revolution. Some of our group were very enthused about what they heard about the ability to elect a person from the block who was then eligible to be elected to the city group and on up to the top. I personally felt cold chills when the chairs of the various committees began to explain their duties. The chair of health care explained, "Castro wants us to be a healthy people, so if your child is having a runny nose and you have not gone to the medics, we will report it so that you will welcome this care." The block group kept repeating, as they translated for us, "We are all workers," and they seemed very proud of their blood donations and the fact that they had picked up a lot of cans. But they told us that the chair of vigilance was to report any wrong-doing on anybody's part. Frightening. The one that did me in was the chair of ideology which they translated as, "I am in charge of how you think." At that point, I got up and started out. Immediately, somebody jumped into the aisle and halted me. I waved my hands in front of my face like a fan and said in poor Spanish, "muy caliente" or very hot. And they let me go outside.

I walked across the street to a one-room mud shed and tried to talk to an elderly lady there. She had a picture of Jesus on the wall. But she told me that the pictures of her children and family had been destroyed.

It made little or no sense to me, but about then, one of the Cubans came and scolded me and told me to get back with my group. Needless to say, I did just that.

On the way out of Cuba, we stopped at a gorgeous beach of snow white sand and a blue Caribbean sea. We had been told not to spend American dollars, but I did. I bought three post cards to send to my children and gave a Cuban a $10 bill to get them out. We have a four generation post card collection in our family, and it includes a card from Cuba back in the 1800s.

Later, my friends told me that I would never see those post cards. But they came—six weeks later. I also purchased a charred picture placed on a piece of wallboard. So I broke the law, but I'm glad.

We issued a statement as a group, and it was a very joyous statement saying that everything was wonderful. I personally disagreed. When we got back to the airport, we found that there were 53 of us and only 52 seats. They asked for a volunteer to wait a week for the next charter. Suddenly, all of those back home appointments became very important and everybody needed to go straight home. I wondered about all of the people that had said in the statement that everything was wonderful. They finally got a volunteer and the church people agreed to get him out later.

While in the airport we watched a quiet and serious group of young Russians re-board a plane, apparently refueling between Nicaragua and Moscow. They were alleged to have delivered a ship of some sort to

Nicaragua. No pleasantries or even smiles were exchanged. We got the benefit of a lot of glares. The last person they put on board was obviously a very inebriated one and his two friends literally dragged him into the plane. We kept trying to smile and speak, but there was no response.

On the way back to the States, I kept thinking of the hymn, "God is Working his Purpose Out," and I kept thinking, "I sure hope so."

Don't Go to Junkanoo

That's the worst advice I ever received. I went to Junkanoo in Nassau on New Year's morning in 1982. And if that was putting my foot back into the petunia bed, I'm glad I did it.

It was around 3 A.M., and our group led by Iris Ann and Grady Cunningham had just saturated ourselves on caviar and sole at the Grey Cliff Restaurant high on a hill, heard the steel drums and danced in the New Year at the Knights and Knaves nightclub. We had been to the Bunny Club at the Ambassador to watch all the folks losing money to start the new year. The casino was doing fine.

We went back to the British Colonial Sheraton—one of the old hotels that looked like it did when the British controlled Nassau as their own. Seven of the guys in our group gathered up their luggage and took off in a limousine for the airport to fly to Fort Lauderdale to fish. That left four women and one guy. We were all exhausted and went back to the hotel.

A taxi driver had told us earlier that the natives paraded and celebrated from 4 A.M. until 9 A.M. They held their celebration late (or early) so that everybody would be off work. The tourists would be through celebrating and be in bed. Our last words from the guys who were leaving were, "Stay in the hotel. Don't go to Junkanoo." We went to the hotel and to our rooms and I was told again, "Stay in the room."

As soon as my friends were out of sight, I went out in front of the hotel. The people were gathering. I wanted to see it. Long single files of natives were headed for Bay Street. A lot of them had on bright colored costumes, similar to ones you might see at Mardi Gras or the Mummer's

Parade in Philadelphia. All of them were talking happily, and some were singing as they walked along. Several of the group carried steel drums of various sizes, and they were thumping them happily as they made their way down the streets. I was just around the corner from Bay Street so I made my way over there rather quickly.

Coming around the corner was a shock. The street was jammed, packed, noisy, and electric. Although the evening was warm and in the low 80s, there were fires on every available vacant lot. The natives seemed to be drawn to them and stood around them happily preening and prancing around in their finery which it had taken most of the year to prepare. The street was filled with native people in bright colored costumes. Some were made of paper, and many were made of a fabric almost like carpet. The colors were bright. Many had shoulder boards, similar to the Mummer Parade, and others had drums. One of the most important symbols was the whistle. The man with the whistle was apparently in charge of each group. He went happily around the street, which was in complete disorder, blowing his whistle. Nobody paid any attention to him.

The crowds on the sidewalk were thick and jammed and slopped over into the street. You couldn't really move on the sidewalk, and if you wanted to get anywhere, you almost had to get off the curb into the street with the performers.

One corner was particularly jammed; it turned out that it was the corner where groups converged from two directions and molded into a "sort-of" parade, nothing like what they show as an orderly assemblage on the post cards named as Junkanoo.

The judges were on a balcony at that corner and that is where everybody was trying to stand. I made a strong attempt to make it to that corner as I filed into that massive crowd. You could feel the anger as I moved through. I wasn't really welcome. A few other watchers had joined me. One of our new group really became afraid and withdrew almost crying, so we all fell back and decided to let them have their corner.

A few more minutes of standing around and watching and listening was enough for the new group. The jungle drums began to thump in a manner that would raise the hairs on your arms. Our group bid for going back to the hotel, although I knew I was coming back out. Somehow, it didn't seem dangerous to me. The people were enjoying it so much.

Back out I came and this time by myself and made my way up the street. I got as close to THE corner as I could manage, which by now was almost a quarter-block away. In front of me was a group of Bahamians dressed like brightly colored tropical birds. Prancing among them was a man in street clothes and a top hat carrying a trophy high in his hand. They were apparently winners from the year before, and he was shaking the trophy in front of each of them as a challenge. Any single costume had probably cost more than the trophy, but the trophy was apparently the envy of everyone on the street.

I found out later that these were the Wylie boys, and they won again. I wasn't surprised. With all that trophy shaking and whistle blowing that was going on in their group, they were really ready for action, by the time they muddled their way up to the judge's corner.

When their drums started, it was a beat that was irresistible. I began to sway to the tempo and a bearded young American in his thirties grabbed my hand and pulled me off the curb, and we began to dance. It was a lot of fun. When the drums slowed down, he leaned over and kissed me on the cheek and said, "You're crazy to be out here, Mom, but I like you. Happy New Year!"

I turned back to the crowd. A small group was having a hard time getting into the action. Their group lacked the professionalism of the Wylie Boys or the sports group that had figures dressed like baseball players or the group that was decked out like policemen. It was apparently a very homemade effort with two guys under a shoulder board, one lone drum, three dancers and only one whistle. They were pushed completely out of the parade four times and once all the way up on the curb into the crowd. They kept threading their way back in and finally became the next to the last group to make it to the judge's corner. I had dubbed them to myself as the Raggedys and watched with interest as they made it up to the corner. They had their small moment of glory as their one lone drum thumped out and the whistler blew his whistle over and over in time to the drum to make a little more noise, and they did their pitiful little dance for the judges. But the feeling was there and nobody laughed as they made their way on by and one side of the shoulder board fell off before they got to the next block. Lots of folks were taking pictures and one drunk young man without a costume kept angrily injecting himself in front of the camera screaming, "I'm a native. Take MY picture."

Tourists were few and more or less ignored and became fewer and fewer as the dawn approached. The people in Nassau make their living catering to the tourists and do so all year with great humbleness and courtesy. This was not their hour to be courteous. This was their party. Most of the tourists who remained were on some type of balcony up above.

The group on the streets became silly with fatigue. The air was clear and that mass of humanity danced on and off the sidewalks up and down the streets, swaying to the drums until dawn. Finally, a fight broke out at one end of the street. Ambulances and sirens seemed to be headed in that direction, so I reluctantly made my way back to the room.

Everybody apparently was running to the fight, and I seemed to be one of the few headed the other way. The parade and dance in the street continued. The drums never ceased.

There were very few children on the street. I don't know where they were because all of their Mamas and Papas were there. There were not too many elderly such as you might see strolling in the daytime, so maybe they stayed home with the babies.

The whole feeling was one of celebration and a hope that maybe this year would be better. It was apparently a symbol like the black-eyed peas in the South. I knew I was to have a New Year without black-eyed peas, but how many ever see a Junkanoo?

The next afternoon at breakfast/lunch, the other members of our group informed me somberly that it was a good thing we got off the street. "We heard ambulances," they said, "They had trouble." I kept eating and clutched to my heart the memory of those hard-working, humble people, cutting free for five hours on a New Year's morning—for Junkanoo.

Celebrating an Inauguration

When I received an invitation to the inauguration of Ronald Reagan as President during his first term, I realized that I didn't really know him, except having covered a couple of occasions where he was present.

But I knew George Bush, who was going in as Vice President, so I wrote his office for press passes or anything I could get so that I could get into things in Washington. I was going to stay with Sarah McClendon and I knew full well that she could get into everything, but not always drag me along.

I had an earlier commitment to speak at a supper at Central Presbyterian Church in Louisville so I spoke and then caught a late plane and got no further than Atlanta that night. I stayed at the motel at the airport and left early as possible—before the sun came up—and went to D. C. I had some passes for the parade and the Vice Presidential reception and a schedule. I had a seat at the inauguration reserved by my Congressman, Charlie Stenholm. But I didn't have an invitation to the Texas breakfast. Right after I landed, I took a taxi to the location of that breakfast anyway. The man at the door was not about to let me in. I was carrying my grip, and it's pretty travel-worn and pitiful. So they looked at it askance. So I asked for Ann Creighton, now Ann Cruz. Ann was press secretary for Governor Bill Clements, and Ann and I used to cover the same wrecks and fires out in West Texas. She then worked at the Midland television station. She came to the door and said, "Of course, she's invited," and took me inside and put me at the table with Alexander Haig who was later named Secretary of State. In fact, he's the one who later tried to take over when Reagan was shot and wounded and he kind of skipped over the Vice President and Speaker of the House in the pecking order.

I remember writing George Bush and saying, "Don't let Haig take over in the next emergency," and George wrote a note back, which I still have, that said, "Pray there is not a next emergency."

Anyway, it was a wonderful breakfast. The hall was decorated with the six flags under which Texas had served. There was Mexican food under the Mexican flag and Spanish food under the Spanish flag, crepes under the French flag, cornbread and grits under the Confederate flag, and so on.

Ann, her parents, and myself and my grip took a taxi on to the Vice President's reception. Fortunately, I had a ticket to that one. But the Secret Service did get a little upset over my suitcase and went through it thoroughly and kept it for me until I left.

I had a really good seat at the inauguration itself and by then I had fortunately gotten my suitcase over to Sarah's house and no longer had to drag it along.

After the inauguration, I took my press pass for the parade and made my way to the designated traffic island. I didn't know what to write on my pass so I had abbreviated Pres. News for Presbyterian News. Of course, it just looked like I couldn't spell Press.

That was an exclusive spot for reporters, and only the major networks and newspapers like The New York Times, The Washington Post, ABC, NBC, CBS, CNN, etc. were there.

They looked at me with great suspicion. In fact, one woman had the Secret Service come over and check my credentials and my camera bag. He told them I had the same credentials they had. They glared at me.

Then Reagan came by in a limo on the side street and whisked on into the main part of the parade. They were standing in an open car and waving. Behind them the Bushes were being whisked. They were also standing up and looking all around at the crowd. Barbara spotted me and hit George on the shoulder and pointed.

One of the big moments of my life was his going around the corner into the main parade and hollering out, "Marj!" Well, my stock went up. The woman who had talked to the Secret Service now came running over to me and said, "Where did you know the Bushes?" I didn't answer. I had no intention of giving her a side comment in her story.

Bush's office had also sent me a pass that after the President and Vice President went by the island, I could leave and walk inside the rope with the parade to take pictures. The woman reporter said, "I've met you before." I still didn't answer. Then she said, "I know where it was. You were at the National Governors' Conference." At that point, I answered in as country, hicky, and rural a tone as I could muster. I said, "No, I don't think so, Honey, becuz I hain't never been to a Guvners' conference in my hull life." And I stepped off that island behind the rope and went off with the parade.

When I got to the National Hotel, I went in and went up to the suite of a friend of Sarah's to watch the rest of the parade. Now each state is allowed one musical group in the parade, and it is selected by the leading politician in that state from the winning party. So Bush had selected the University of Texas band, and Lamar Alexander had selected the University of Tennessee band. They both wore orange and white. They were right together in the parade, since it was in alphabetical order by states. The two bands came marching by looking like one big band playing two different fight songs. It was hilarious.

Before the parade ended, the announcement came that the hostages had been freed in the Middle East, and balloons went up from the White House, and everybody cheered and cried.

The wonderful day was not over. Sarah and I got on the last bus to the Gala out in Maryland. There were only eight of us on that bus, including a reporter from the National Observer who was very snooty. But it also included a wonderfully friendly Jamie Auchincloss, who was Jackie Kennedy's half-brother.

What a day—one I'll never forget, although a time or two that day my foot was back in the petunias.

Into the Water I Went

In March, 1999, Six Flags Over Texas suffered its first fatality in over forty years as an amusement park. When a raft collapsed, several were hurt, and one woman was drowned.

It made me think back to 1963 and count my blessings. Because I went into the water at Six Flags that spring.

Maureen Whitley, Kate Hall, Billie Bickley, a couple of other volunteer mothers, and I took Girl Scouts to Six Flags. We slept in bedrolls on the floor at the Arlington Scout Hut. We divided up into the buddy system at Six Flags.

Maureen and I were watching my son, Jim Bob, who was seven years old at the time. The girls were off on their own. Somehow when we got to one of the islands, we lost Jim Bob. I was frantically calling and looking everywhere. I stepped out onto a buckling bridge. About that time, somebody stepped on either end of it, and it buckled up into the air; I went over into the drink.

I remember trying to hold the camera out of the water, but my head went all the way under. As it wasn't too deep there and when my feet touched bottom, I kind of waded and pushed back to where my head was out. By then a couple attendants were into the water trying to help me. They say now they are not allowed to do this. I was kind of glad to see them. Maureen was on the bridge all upset. I handed her the camera. I felt in the pocket of my dress for my billfold; it was soggy but there. I was helped out. There stood Jim Bob with his eyes real big. He had heard the commotion and come on over to the spot. I said to him angrily, "I was looking everywhere for you." And he answered calmly, "I wasn't in the water."

I took the camera to the shop. They took out the film and developed it. It was fine, but the camera was forever ruined. It was full of mud and gravel. It belonged to The Pecos Independent newspaper, and they weren't too thrilled over that. I thought they'd be thrilled that I had not drowned, but they seemed to be more concerned with their camera.

The only ill effects that I had was I got a terrible earache that afternoon. Maureen took me to the infirmary where they gave me some medication and put me on a cot to rest. I went to sleep for a couple hours and left everybody else to deal with the Girl Scouts.

Those girls were used to me being a disaster. I worked with most of them eight or ten years. They took it calmly that the dye in the water had given me the earache.

After all, when we hiked up to see the Indian paintings near Mitre Peak in the Davis Mountains in Texas, I was the only one who slipped and fell. I peeled my leg and told them, "We will now have a lesson in first aid. Bring the first aid box."

That group of over forty girls turned out to be some of the finest young women I know all over the country. It made me believe in scouting. If I could have that kind of success in spite of slipping down mountains and falling in the water, I know that it's alright if you get your foot in the durn petunias.

A Day to Remember

We all have days from our lives that are indelibly imprinted on our minds and hearts. One of those for me is March 29th. That is the day that Billie Sol Estes was arrested by the FBI in Pecos, Texas. The year was 1962. The time was about 7 P.M.

At The Pecos Independent, we had been edgy for days as more and more representatives from financial institutions that had loaned money to Estes showed up on our doorstep. One of them was particularly dramatic because it was a small company, and the downfall of Estes was going to ruin them.

We knew the FBI was into the act. I remember at the post office that morning, I ran across a man who was a very good friend of Estes. He also was working with the girls' softball league in Pecos in which my two daughters were involved. One of my girls was on the Estes ball team, the Black Panthers. My other daughter was on the Green Hornets and was sponsored by a barber shop. Now, the barber shop had paid their $100 fee, but Estes had not yet put money into the league. I asked the friend, "Did you get Billie Sol's money for the baseball team?" "Not yet," he replied, "There's no hurry." "Oh," I answered, "There might be. If I were you, I'd get it today." He laughed, "Are you trying to tell me that because of those silly articles your paper has been running, somebody is going to arrest Billie Sol Estes?" I simply answered, "If I were you, I'd get it today." He laughed all the way out of the post office. That was Charlie Smith. The night before at a PTA meeting at Pecos Elementary, Nelva Foster and I were hostesses, preparing the refreshments. Nelva's husband, A.B., was

Estes' bookkeeper. He came to help us clean up. He absent mindedly stuck Nelva's electric percolator down in the dish water. She screamed at him, "You're ruining the coffee pot!" I remember he looked over at me and said quietly, "I wish that was all I had to worry about."

It was a terrible time. Reporters began to come in from Associated Press in Dallas; Jimmy Banks from the Dallas Morning News and Clyde Walters from the Amarillo newspaper were there.

I was assigned that night to go cover the initial meeting of the new board of a women's chamber of commerce. So, that's where I was at the time Estes was arrested. I was arguing with a civic leader who said, "Marj, your newspaper (and it wasn't my newspaper) has been tearing up the town. And nobody is paying any attention to them. Why don't they just shut up?" The phone rang. It was for me . . . Oscar Griffin, our city editor, said, "Marj, they've just arrested Estes. Be sure your kids are all right, and then get down to the Federal Building and get a picture of him coming out with the Deputy Marshall.

I remember turning to Alton Hughes and saying, "Well, somebody was paying attention after all." And I walked out. I went by the house and told my children to lock the doors and not to answer the door no matter how loud people rang. I also told them not to answer the telephone no matter how many times it rang. I felt sorry for them, but that was the best I could do at that point.

It was a frightening evening for us all. I went back to the post office and waited until they brought Estes out. I took a couple pictures and then watched in fascination as a real pro photographer from the Dallas Morning News leaped around getting pictures, literally getting right under his feet to take a close-up.

I went back to check on the kids and then went to the paper. We put out an extra that night—the only one I remember at that newspaper.

I got home late and tired. As I got out of my car in front of the house, a car zoomed forward and almost sideswiped my car. I pulled back in, or I would have been mashed.

The next day I got the kids off to school. My husband was furious about the whole thing. The kids had a terrible day. Cathy was in junior high, and they were celebrating April Fool's Day by coming in costume. Days before we had dressed her as a newspaper. So that's the way she went, and it was a bad day to be a newspaper. On the way home after school, Jim Bob was just a block from the house when he was run up on the curb by what he called "a big, black car full of men" who picked him up and took him to the newspaper where I worked, let him out, and said, "tell your mother about this", and drove away. I was extremely frightened because I didn't know who they were.

Yes, I remember March 29, 1962, although it's been many years ago as I write this. It was a terrible day from which many of my friends and acquaintances and the town itself have never recovered.

The Rat and I

There was a large group of us traveling together in different parts of Africa, and one of the places we went was Kananga, Zaire, in the area where the Good Shepherd Hospital is located and also a seminary and churches.

We split up and stayed in homes. There aren't exactly any motels around there. I ended up in the home of Angie Anderson, a wonderful missionary who did really fine work in that area.

I'd had a long day and had supper and was ready to go to bed, wherever and whatever the bed might be. It was a cot with a nightstand and lamp next to it. Just as I was about to go to sleep, having turned off the light, I realized something was looking at me, and I saw the bright red eyes of a huge rat on the night stand. I sat up suddenly, tried to keep from screaming and turned on the lamp. The rat fled.

Evidently, he doesn't like light, I thought. I hated to leave Angie's lamp on all night, and I tried to decide what to do. I found my flashlight and propped it up and turned it on. Then, I took my precious half a canteen of boiled water and added some of my precious Scotch. I thought if there ever was a time that I needed it, it was that night. I drank it. I let the flashlight burn. I pulled the covers over my head and thought, "Goodnight, Mr. Rat."

The next morning, Bill Patton came over for breakfast. He said, "I am so tired, Marj. I didn't get to stay in a missionary home like you did. I stayed at the home of one of the native people, and I saw a rat in my room, so I got up and walked all night long."

"Well," I said, "Bill, I hate to tell you that rats don't choose between natives and missionaries. I saw a rat in my room, too. And I slept fine.

But you should be thankful because the missionary Mattoxes tell me that they've killed cobras outside their home. You were out there walking around in the dark." Bill looked ill.

Little do we know what our mission workers put up with around the world. And unfortunately, one of the things they put up with is us Presbyterian guests. They may prefer the rats.

They Tell You Where to Go

When after five months of trying, I obtained a visa into North Korea during my year as Moderator of the 205th General Assembly of the Presbyterian Church (USA), I was really happy.

I flew to San Francisco and then China because you cannot go from South Korea to North Korea. Then I flew with one of our church leaders, the Rev. Syngman Rhee on into North Korea.

They met us and took our picture for the newspaper. They took our umbrellas away, and it was pouring so we looked like two drowned rats.

I was ready to pick up my luggage but we were met by government representatives who said, "Sit there, and we get the luggage." That was my first realization that I wasn't exactly going to be free to run around North Korea.

They drove us in a big, black Mercedes, a government car, to a government guest house. I was showed to my quarters and every time I stepped out of them, night or day, a government man rose from the chair outside the door and said, "Where are we going?"

And go we did. The first place we went was to the gigantic statue of "our great leader" who was now dead. They gave me a spray of beautiful flowers and said I was to leave them at the foot of the statue and bow my head, and I did so. I wasn't too thrilled over this, but it didn't seem like a good time to argue about it. So, I did it.

As I bowed my head, I thought of a Korean friend I had back in Kansas City who is a professor at a college there. He said when Japan occupied

Korea when he was a lad, they made them bow to Shintu. His grandmother told him not to do that—that he was Christian. He said as they towered over him and offered rather severe beatings if you didn't bow, he prayed to God to forgive him and told God, "When I bow and place my hands as in prayer, I will spit into my hands, and then, it doesn't count."

I gave some thought to spitting into my hands but decided that wasn't worth it either. It had taken five months to get there. I didn't want to get thrown out before I could see the church.

We went to see where our great leader had lived. We went to see where his grandmother lived. We went to see where he went to school. I brightened up at that point and told them, "This was a Presbyterian mission school." They didn't think too much of that, but it was true. We educated "their great leader."

They took us to the hospitals. At a children's hospital, we saw a darling set of triplets. They said preemies stay three months until they are healthy and go home. It is all free. I pondered that awhile.

We went to a library, and Sygnman ran over to look at the dictionary. He came back smiling. He was raised in North Korea and had made earlier trips into that country. He had argued with the great leader about them having taken the word Christianity out of the dictionary. It was back, and he was happy.

Finally, on Easter Sunday, we were allowed to go to two of the three Christian churches in the entire country. In Pyongyang, there is one Catholic and two Protestant churches. These were opened with permission of the leader before he died. His mother had been an active Presbyterian.

I went first to the Catholic church to take greetings. There was poor attendance, and they were obviously struggling. They were not allowed to have a priest because that would tie them to the West.

We went to the larger Protestant church, and I was praying there would be people there. It was full to the walls, with people outside. They aren't allowed to be "tied to the West" either, but there is a difference.

The Presbyterians had an active seminary in Pyongyang for over fifty years and so there are a lot of ordained preachers still alive, and two of them were leading that congregation.

It was a Presbyterian Easter service in the Korean language. You could tell as they sang, "Christ the Lord is Risen Today" and "How Great Thou Art" in Korean.

The question and answer period afterward was heartbreaking. I answered a lot of questions. The hardest one was from a woman in back who said, "Is there still a church in the world? Where is it?"

After the questions, we made a circle and sang, "God Be with You till We Meet Again", and we all wept.

Even the government driver was strangely silent.

And The Embassy Was Closed

It was an interesting trip. We were a mixed group of Presbyterians representing the Presbyterian Church U.S., and we were to make a report on Central America for the next General Assembly. I was taken along simply because they thought I could write.

When we boarded the plane in Miami, I had never heard of the city I was en route to visit. The attendant said, "Are you going to Tegucigalpa?" And I answered, "Whatever it says on that ticket, that's where I'm going." She looked startled.

I was to write a brief paragraph about each country we visited for the report of the committee. I still have those photographs. The one about Honduras read as follows:

"A preacher for a Pentecostal denomination in Honduras stood in an office in Tegucigalpa and talked in earnest tones. His face was almost pure Mayan in structure and his voice was calm and slow. He and others sitting with him were from denominations that in the States would be considered conservative and evangelical. But this young man was taking a strong stand for social action—a strong stand against the world as he knew it." "It is our place in history to work for the people." "His voice remained soft and controlled and his face held the calm of the Mayan race. But there were those in the room who knew that his life was in danger because of the work he does with both refugees and the poor within the land. He put his action behind his soft-spoken words."

Across the street from that office was a former office where they used to meet. The front door of that building was riddled with bullet holes. It was not a safe country. We stayed out of town in a camp, either for safety or Presbyterian frugality—I never was sure which.

We visited the embassy. On the next day, we were leaving and went together to the airport. Next, we were going to Nicaragua. I was first in line and went through customs fairly easily and on into the waiting area. Only one other member of the group came through behind me. There was a long period of nobody coming. Something had gone wrong.

I peered out from behind bars and saw two of our group, Jorge LaraBrau and Gaspar Langello down below walking around holding suitcases over their heads. I thought that was weird. I started calling out their names.

One came up and told me through the bars, "They have detained Richard Siciliano." He was a pastor and presbytery executive from Houston. "Why are you holding suitcases on your heads?" I asked. "Because they are filming us from up above," they answered. "What happened, anyway?" I asked. "Well," Gaspar said, "Apparently, he did something stupid. Someone in Washington, D.C., had given him pictures of the Honduran Air Force and he brought them with him and had them in his brief case. And since we're on the way to Nicaragua and those countries are presently enemies, he's in big trouble." "Did you call the American Embassy?" I asked. "Yes," they answered, "But this is Columbus Day, and that's a big holiday here so the embassy is closed." They continued, "We sent for some of the church leaders, and they are coming. We may need you to come out and telephone Associated Press in the States and see if we can shake him loose with the threat of a big story." "All right," I said, "I have a number. Just tell me when . . ."

In the area in which I was located, there was a bar, and I headed for it. I sat and watched for more of our group. Dotty Bernard, former moderator of the PCUS, came through and said, "Maybe I should fly on to Nicaragua and report," she stated. I answered, "I really think we should all stay here until they release Dick."

Next, Emily Wood came through. She was crying. She said, "They took all the papers out of our luggage. They said they were communistic. They may be, but they are in Spanish, and I can't even read them."

Others came through—Dick Junkin, Ben Guttierez, Bob Brashear, Vernon Broyles, Alicia Martinez, Margaret Montgomery . . . I can't remember them all. It's been a number of years back.

I sat quietly holding a Scotch and water. One of the group said, "Aren't you going to drink it?" and I answered, "No, I'm saving it for Dick. I think they'll release him at the last moment, and he's going to need it."

That's exactly what happened. And as he came through looking extremely pale, I handed him that Scotch, and he drank it in one swallow. We got on the plane. They changed our seat assignments. A Honduran sat by Dick and began to question him again. He started to answer. I leaned back and said, "Dick, we're still in Honduran air space. You look tired. Why don't you go to sleep?" And he shut his eyes. The Honduran glared at me.

Gaspar later put in the report of the church, "When many of us were rattled, Marj Carpenter handled herself with aplomb." I wasn't sure what aplomb was, but it sounded good.

But the embassy was closed.

And there I was with a group that all had their feet in the petunias.

Dick said they requested all of our names. He added, "I would have given them the names of every Presbyterian in Houston if they wanted them, but I forgot one of our group." "I hope it was me," I stated. "No," he answered. "It was Dick Junkin. You were the first one I put down."

About Visiting Jails

Did you ever visit even one jail? It gives you a strange feeling. I've been into many jails, and they certainly vary.

My first experiences with "going to jail" were small West Texas town jails. I often was down there at various sheriff's offices, plugging to get the kids out that I didn't think were criminals.

I remember one night in Andrews, Texas, that the sheriff's deputies were busy because a rock band had come to town along with a lot of college kids and a lot of beer in that dry county. The deputies were rushing around all night warning kids and watching kids and trying to keep them all safe. They found one young boy and girl passed out on the grass of the football field and took them to jail. Some other teenagers came to get me and told me who they had jailed. The kids were from Mentone, a very small town about fifty miles away.

I went in to ask the sheriff to release them to me, and he said, "Why?" I said, "Just last week, these two kids watched a small plane crash on their ranch and kill both their parents. I think they are just upset . . . not criminals." He turned them loose in my company, and I got some of their friends to take them on home.

There were a lot of similar incidents, and you don't want to read them all. There was one Halloween night in Big Spring when some teenagers decided to stop and take some of the candy away from the little kids. The little kids set up a howl, and the police arrested the teenagers for attempting kidnapping. I went to the city jail to get them out and explain they were snitching candy, not kids.

I've also visited in federal prisons, and at one point in my career, I also rode an old school bus with a Baptist youth choir that went across Texas singing in all the prisons. That trip got scary at times. There was one women's prison where, right after they sang, somebody came in and told an inmate that she had a visitor. I learned later that she had been there fifteen years and never once had a visitor. She let out a blood-curdling scream. Then, all the prisoners got very restless. It was frightening. I remember helping hustle that group of teenager choir members out of a side door quickly.

But the worst prisons are not in America. They're in the poor countries. My friend Lydia Hernandez and I went into a Reynosa, Mexico, jail one time to see if there were any Salvadorian refugees being locked up.

A young man from Florida, barefoot, and bare chested with just his blue jeans on, came running over, rattled the bars and asked, "Do you speak English? Can you get me a lawyer?" We talked to him. They had taken away his clothes. He told us that prisoners didn't get to eat in that jail unless somebody brought food. A Mexican inmate had been sharing the food that was brought by his wife. We told the youth that if they thought he had money for a lawyer, he was doomed. He had been arrested asleep near the road. He had come down to Mexico on a toot after getting a divorce from a very early marriage. Lydia talked to the warden and told him the boy had no money, no family, and no friends. "How much have you spent on him?" she asked. "About $20," they replied. I gave them $30, and they released him. We took him back to the Texas side of the border, gave him a little money, and let him out of the car. They had given him back his shirt and shoes, but of course, he had lost his billfold. I remember him saying, "I never went to church, but if I ever do, it will be Presbyterian." He waved, and we were gone.

Down in Buenos Aires, I walked with the mothers who circle in front of the Pink House every Wednesday. That's the same as our White House. They know they will never see their sons again, but they want to know what happened to them. It was an emotional and quiet demonstration which happens there every week.

In Brazil, one of our missionaries was taking strong human rights stands in that country years ago. His name was Jim Wright. His brother was also taking strong stands and was taken to jail. Nobody ever saw him again. It's scary stuff.

In Nicaragua, there was a new concept in jails in one location. There was an open jail 23 kilometers from Managua and almost all of the 282 prisoners were former National guardsmen who fought with Samoza. When the Sandinistas took over, they jailed them rather than killing them as had been the normal practice following most revolutions in the Central and South American countries.

One young man, who had been an officer, told us of getting his wife and children on a plane to the States the day before the country fell. He hid three days before giving himself up. He had been jailed since July 23, 1979. He was head of discipline in the camp, which included men working as mechanics, carpenters, and some were weaving hammocks. One man leaned against a shed while we were there holding an open Bible and reading the 23rd Psalm. I had this sinking feeling that it was staged.

The hope of the prisoners at that time was that their terms might be shortened, and they could again join their families and fit into the society of Nicaragua, a country which they love.

One poster picture often seen in Managua at that time showed a mother of a young man killed in a recent border skirmish. The poster said, "National guard mothers, your son is in jail. Where is my son?"

Jails are varied. Jails are terrible. If you've never visited a jail, you've missed a heart-rending experience.

George Bush's Big Day

I returned to Washington, D.C., for the George Bush presidential inauguration. Again, I stayed with Sarah McClendon, and again, I had a wonderful seat at the inauguration itself from my Congressman. I was sitting alongside some bishops from the Greek Orthodox Church, and we all had a good time.

Afterward, Sarah and I got back together and caught the Metro to a location where she said we were invited to a party that had a good view of the parade. After my previous experience with reporters on the street eight years earlier, I was ready to go to a room with a view.

Having attended a few inaugurations, I have learned that each region, North, South, East, and West, has a float, and that's all the floats that are allowed. It is primarily a musical group parade with one from each state.

When we got to the party room where we could see the parade, I was really enjoying it, and when the float came by from the West, I kind of went crazy. I had no idea that Bush had selected the Jody Nix band from Big Spring, Texas, to ride that float and play Bob Wills songs. Jody's father, Hoyle, used to play with the original Bob Wills band. Jody operates a place called the Stompede in Big Spring, and that is THE place to go. Bob Wills and Hoyle Nix have gone on to that country western section somewhere in the sky, but Jody is still there.

After watching for a while, I left the party room to go down the hall to the restroom and when returning, got back into the wrong room. They all looked alike. I got chewed out soundly by some little lady from Indiana. It seems I was in the Birch Bayh room, instead of whatever room Sarah had originally taken me to. It took me a little while and a lot of opening and closing of doors to find my correct spot again.

The next day, I went along to the White House press room with Sarah. I was sitting there minding my own business and waiting for her to get through, when they announced that President Bush was coming out on the White House lawn with the grandchildren, and it was a "photo opportunity." Cameramen leaped up everywhere. Well, I had a little camera with me, so I leaped up, too, and went out on the lawn. It was a little uphill to where Bush was to appear, and I panted and puffed getting up that hill. I was the last one to get to the top so everybody had already gathered all around Bush so you couldn't even get close to him. I didn't even try. I just stood back.

Then, he got a little bit peeved and went back inside and sent word out by the Secret Service that he'd come back out, but they were not to cross a line so people could get pictures of his grandchildren. Then, I got a little closer as they were coming out. I suddenly saw George Walker Bush, later Governor of Texas and then, President, and I hollered, "George—Young George . . ." He looked up and waved and smiled and hit his Dad on the shoulder and said, "There's Marj from Big Spring." By then I was from Louisville, Kentucky, but who cared? The newly-installed President of the United States came over to me and said, "Marj, I'm glad you're here." And I answered, "And I'm glad you're here." He laughed and walked away.

My stock went up again like it had eight years before when Barbara got his attention. This time it was his son who helped me out. Reporters asked me where I knew him, and I answered, "As a matter of fact, in a place where some of you said that he never lived—West Texas."

By then, Sarah had finished filing her story and came looking for me. She was worried about me. Country girl come to town—she'll get her foot in the petunias again . . .

Then, she said that she noticed Bush was over talking to me, and the other reporters were back behind the line, so she quit worrying.

It was a wonderful day—a beautiful day—and I enjoyed every minute of it.

About Covering Plane Crashes

Most people are fortunate enough never to have had to come close to a plane crash in their lifetime. I'm fortunate enough never to have come close to a major airliner crash in my lifetime.

But I have been to many small plane crashes. And there are many in West Texas. West Texas and Alaska probably have more private planes than anywhere in the world because of the distances people have to travel.

I remember one crash outside Andrews, Texas, one night. The plane really plowed deep into the earth. The pilot had taken off in Hobbs, New Mexico, and apparently became completely unconscious. My fourteen year old son insisted on going along with me that night, and I think he wished that he hadn't done that. It was gruesome. It was more difficult for me because I knew the family of the victim.

I remember another night when a plane crashed outside Big Spring, Texas. I went to that location with my Cuban photographer friend, Danny Valdes. We were walking in the dark across a plowed field to get to the scene of the crash. Danny suddenly said, "We should have brought a flashlight. There are rattlesnakes out here this time of night . . ." That almost did me in. From then on, I was walking with my head down, watching very carefully where I stepped.

On another night, Danny and I went to a train wreck outside Big Spring. We had to crawl through the train to the other side to get the pictures and talk to the investigators. I remember being very uneasy and afraid that the train would start about the time we went across it.

Another memory is of a private plane crash outside Pecos, Texas. One of my daughters was in the car and went along with me. She was wandering around and picked up something to show me. I screamed at her. "Drop it. Get back in the car. Don't touch another thing. That's the top of somebody's head." She scurried off in fright and got in the car and rolled up the windows.

Another time, in Mentone, Texas, I remember a plane crash where the children saw their parents in a small plane that was landing. It crashed and burned.

At another time, a plane crashed at the Andrews airport while the family stood in the front yard watching their husband and father attempt to land.

I remember too many, and just like the car wrecks, they are terrible, but they are part of covering news in areas like West Texas.

Several years later when traveling with the church, I stayed in a Presbyterian home in North Pole, Alaska. That family owned a car, a pickup, a small plane, and a seaplane with a water strip on which to land. This was normal for them. I remember thinking, "Oh, my goodness . . ."

Actually, there are more car crashes percentage-wise than plane crashes. But the plane crashes leave the victims with such a helpless feeling, according to the few who survive. It was definitely one of the more difficult tasks of covering West Texas news.

When I was moderator of the Presbyterian Church, I was at Fort Bragg, North Carolina, visiting with chaplains at that base. Somebody came to get one of them. A captain had done a practice parachute jump. His chute failed. That should have been all right because there is an emergency chute, but it also failed.

I remember feeling great sympathy for the chaplain who had to go and tell his family of the disaster. Life can really be tragic.

And Military Airplane Crashes

When I was covering Webb Air Force Base at Big Spring, Texas, for the Big Spring Herald, there were three air crashes rather close together that I covered for news.

One of them was on a ranch out in Borden County. John Edwards, a fellow reporter, and I drove out there. We climbed through a barbed wire fence. I took pictures and for some reason took the film out of the camera and put it in my bra. I had an uneasy feeling because the military wasn't there yet. We had heard the report on the police radio and beaten them to the scene.

As we were returning, a group of military vehicles headed by a highway patrol car ran us off the road into a ditch. I thought for a minute they thought we were Bonnie and Clyde. John hadn't stopped soon enough to suit them, and they got rather aggressive.

Bill Priest, the patrolman, knew me, and he said, "Marj, give me your camera." I obliged. He opened it, and it was empty. "Marj, I need the film," he said angrily. I answered, "You can't have it. It's on my person, and you do not have any female officers with you. Call my editor and talk to him. When I get back to the paper, he will decide along with your military officials what happens to the film." John started up the engine, and we drove off.

When we got to the paper, Joe Pickle, the managing editor said, "Marj, where is the film?" I pulled it out from its hiding place. He laughed. "That's where they said it was," and he turned to Danny Valdes who ran our dark room and said, "Print it. It's not war time. It's not a military secret. It's

127

news." And we ran the pictures. They were not as good as if Danny had been there to go along, but they were printable.

The Webb Air Force Base public relations officer was Dick Risk, a captain, and he was unhappy. He put together a film strip and invited all the reporters—newspapers, radio, and television in the West Texas area—to attend a briefing on proper protocol. We were shown pictures of reporters being put in the brig or whatever they called it. The pictures were obviously made back in war time. We didn't pay a whole lot of attention to it.

The next crash was on a local ranch a little closer to town. I had just been injured a few weeks before when a pickup truck attempted to run over me after I had covered a union meeting. I was wearing a back brace. I had a cast on my left arm all the way up to the shoulder.

When Danny Valdes and I started into that field to get pictures, I was limping with a cane. Captain Risk was backing up in front of us saying, "No. No. No." But what are you going to do about stopping a little old lady in a back cast with a broken arm and limping along with a cane?

About then the rancher came along and said, "This is my ranch and your airplane. They can take pictures of your plane on my ranch if they want to . . ." And we did.

A third time, one of the Iranian students on his first solo flight got frightened, ejected, and let a very expensive jet plane go to earth. He wasn't hurt.

We rushed out to yet another ranch and were trying to get a picture of the pilot, but Captain Risk slammed the door of the ambulance. We could see the pilot was unhurt and just sitting there.

Well, you can't win them all. But those were extremely interesting days.

An interesting side note is that years later, Captain Risk was working for an oil company in Tulsa and saw in the local newspaper that I was preaching at a Tulsa church. He came to hear me and said he absolutely could not believe that I was preaching.

Somebody asked me once how I can have covered all of those plane crashes and still fly as much as I do. My answer is simple, "I trust in the Lord."

Stories That I Can't Forget

Some people believe that all lawmen and all reporters get hardhearted and have no sympathy for victims. This is simply not so. We bury it and try not to dwell on it. But there are many stories that you never forget, no matter how hard you try.

One of those occurred in Pecos, Texas, when the Tudor family went home for lunch. They were a close family and enjoyed having lunch together. The three children were at the kitchen table, and the mother was getting something out of the icebox. The father had just driven up out front. A soft drink delivery truck lost its brakes on a curve and ran through the house—right over the kitchen table and killed all three children. One lived a few hours. The mother was pinned to the wall. The father was, of course, hysterical. It was just unbelievable—and awful. She had all "c-section births" and had been told not to have any more children, but eventually, they did have two other children. What faith! What love!

Then, I remember in Balmorhea, Texas, there was a farmer who lived across the highway from his wife's parents. One day, their three-year-old simply decided to go see Grandma and walked out on that highway and was killed. A horrible story.

I remember being at a girl scout meeting and getting a call from the police dispatcher that there had been a fatality involving a school bus out on the highway to Toyah. I left the troop with the assistant and took off. I saw the lights blinking on the back of the bus for miles before I got there. It had stopped and let out a little girl. When she stepped in front of the bus to cross the road where her mother was waiting, a car, later determined to be going about 90 miles per hour, struck the child, threw her way up in the air, and killed her.

The second tragedy was yet to occur. The mother did not understand. She was completely wiped out and decided to get drunk. She had never drunk whiskey. She bought a bottle and drank it all; she died of alcoholic poisoning.

I remember in Big Spring, Texas, the photographer and I were called to a double death. An elderly couple had walked out of the house holding an old steel umbrella to get in the car and go to a funeral. Lightning struck the tip of the umbrella and killed them both.

There was a young lad in Pecos, Texas, named Burl Holloway who wanted to work in the oilfields to make a little money. His father said that it wasn't safe for a young boy so instead, he got a job chopping cotton. It wasn't even raining, but lightning struck the ID tags he wore around his neck and killed him. Who can understand that one?

And one of the worst—one which used to haunt me. An elderly woman in Big Spring went out in the backyard on a hot summer day and had a stroke. She lay in the yard without being able to summon help. Fire ants literally killed her.

I remember two small boys who were eating Thanksgiving dinner at their aunt's house in Mercedes, Texas. They went out in the yard to play. They wandered down the road to the canal, and Donny came back and told the others, "Bobby is gone—under the water."

Tragedies—tragedies all. And yes, they do bother me A lot.

Where is Cochabamba and Where is Marj?

In August, 1997, I decided to visit Bolivia along with my church friend, Lois Hall from Fernandino Beach in Florida. We had originally planned to go on a planned trip with the hunger committee, but they seemed to think for some reason I would die in that high altitude and kept yammering about me getting a special physical.

I got angry enough that we decided to just go on our own. So I contacted a former missionary to Bolivia, and he gave me the name of a Christian there who spoke English, and I made my contacts.

We did not realize that the day we selected to leave the country was election day in La Paz. We were held up in Miami by the airlines who gave all kinds of excuses—never saying it was because it was election day. But they put us up in a motel, and we were to go the next day.

We thought nothing of it, having traveled a lot, and many things happen along the way. But the Christians meeting the plane in La Paz kept meeting planes and meeting planes and got all upset. A young woman from San Antonio, Texas, who was serving in some capacity down there decided to call the Presbyterian headquarters in Louisville.

Well, since they weren't sending me, I hadn't even told them when I was going. So they called my daughter in the publications department where she edited books, and she got all upset. She called her brother and sister. Her brother got particularly upset. He called the hotel in La Paz, and they spoke only Spanish and hung up on him. He called his Congressman.

He called the State Department. He called the airlines who reported that they had gotten us to Santa Cruz, but then we didn't appear on the next plane to La Paz. They didn't know where we were.

Well, they should of, because they put us on the wrong plane and sent us to Cochabamba. We got off there and thought we were in La Paz and asked for our luggage. They told us that we were not in La Paz. "You're in Cochabamba." I asked, "What country is that in?" And they answered, "Bolivia." I said, "Well, at least we are in the right country."

We shopped in the airport and finally were put on a plane to La Paz.

In the meantime, back in the states, my son had found a fellow employee where he worked who spoke Spanish; he was going to take him with him and fly to La Paz and start hunting for me. The State Department asked my daughter for a description of me; I really don't want to know how she described me.

We got to La Paz. They were still having a lot of commotion in the streets. Soldiers were literally goose-stepping like the old Nazi armies up the street. Some people were celebrating and dancing. We didn't have any luggage yet, but we went to the hotel and went to bed.

The next day, the luggage appeared, right at the doorway of our room. Then, the Christians appeared and told us of all the turmoil. Then, I called home and told my daughter, we were all right.

But once again, I had my foot in the durn petunias. Without even meaning to do so, I had caused all kinds of commotion.

Well, we had a wonderful time. We visited little adobe churches on the sides of hills that they were about to slide off. We went to the highest lake in the world and ate fish. We got out of a broken down van in a snow storm, and we just had a marvelous experience.

Even with all of the commotion, I'd do it again. And again. And again. And I didn't have any health problems.

Favorite Reporters

When you work as a reporter, you run across a lot of competitive reporting and a lot of jealousy. But sometimes, you run across reporters you really like and enjoy working with most of the time.

I've been lucky enough to know several of these. One was Jimmy Banks from the Dallas Morning News, who worked on the Estes scandal. He was definitely my favorite at that time. Some of the others were good reporters; however, some of them cow-towed to Estes, trying to get an inside track. Some listened at doors. Everybody wasn't ethical, but most were.

Oscar Griffin at The Pecos Independent was great to work with. He went on to win the Pulitzer Prize, and he deserved it. The paper also nominated three of us as a team, but they awarded it to the individual, which was all right with me.

In corresponding for other newspapers, I had three favorites. Two of them were in San Angelo. They were Dale Walton and Ross McSwain. Both were crackerjack reporters and always kind to the correspondents. Dale kept a special file on me because he thought they were going to find me dead in a ditch. I was glad he never had to use it. He ended up as managing editor out in Tucson where he later retired. I asked him what he did with the file; he said he left it in San Angelo.

Ross later worked for the Wool and Mohair Association and also has written books. He is constantly on call in West Texas to do even more.

The other reporter I enjoyed was Bill Birge on The El Paso Times. He used to kid me that he was a cousin or second cousin of Ladybird's. When

I would call in a story, I would always ask for Cousin Billy. Unfortunately, he dropped dead while in Juarez, Mexico, and fell off a bar stool.

In Big Spring, I worked well with Jamie Werrell and Bob Burton, both of whom had come from back East at Colgate and Beloit Universities and had a lot to learn about West Texas. But they learned.

And my personal favorite of all time was Danny Valdes, a Cuban photographer for the Big Spring Herald. We went about covering news together quite often. He'd take the pictures. I'd get the story. He was a wonderful photographer. He won a lot of AP awards.

One of them was for the Kentucky Fried chicken truck that fell off the bridge onto the railroad. He called me at 4 A.M. and said in his Cuban accent, "There's shicken on the ground. They're giving it away before it thaws. It's still frozen and all cut up and everything." So, away we went. I had a very hard time getting back up the hill from the wreck with that "shicken". I told my youth group Sunday School class that morning that I wondered if I would have been able to get home with the "manna on the ground."

When my son came home from the University of Texas that weekend, I had fried up a platter of chicken. He knew I didn't like to fry chicken. "What got into you?" he asked. And I answered, "Well, there was "shicken" on the ground."

One of the saddest statements I ever heard Danny make was one that he made when I was at their home visiting his wife, Norma, and children, Ileana, Alex, and Danny. He said, "I have lost two things in my life that I regret. One was my son (who had died of leukemia), and one was my country (Cuba)."

Going about with Danny was interesting. People got where they watched for his little, yellow Volkswagen. When he took pictures, he would invariably say, "One, two, three, sheeeese." And everybody would smile.

One time when he got stuck, I had to get out and push. And one time, he persuaded me to walk through a ditch of shallow water to see if I thought the Volkswagen would make it.

The Monarch butterflies fly through Big Spring each year, migrating south, and they always stop at certain trees and completely cover the trees for a few days while they rest. Danny went out to take a picture, and all of the butterflies were asleep with their wings folded. He talked me into jumping up and down under the tree so the butterflies would flutter, and he would get a better picture. He got a prize-winning picture with that one.

We covered wrecks, house parties, grassfires, oilfield fires, plane crashes, train crashes, Webb Air Force base, football games, and all other sports, political rallies, style shows, chamber banquets, school events, musicals, entertainment stars, rodeos, and endless ribbon cutting ceremonies. It was the most interesting newsbeat I ever had. I wrote about everything from macaroni to murder.

Is This a New Chinese Word?

A trip through China, back at the time when it first opened up for travelers, and tourists were able to visit, was very interesting and exciting.

There was a large group of Presbyterians, including several former missionaries and their children who went back to China on this trip. The Tommy Browns were the group leaders. They had lived in China and really knew the territory.

The large group naturally broke into small groups, and there were four of us who ran around together to view the sights. In fact, we became known as the gang of four. It was Bob Gray from Florida, David Burr from North Carolina, Mabel Franz from Texas, and myself.

By the time we got to Hong Kong near the end of the trip, we had already visited Beijing, Quelin, Nanjing, Shanghai, Canton, and many other places. We had eaten a lot of strange things and seen a lot of wonderful things. And we were really ready for some western food.

We were walking rapidly to a well-known hotel in Kowloon and were quite excited about it. Somehow, Mabel and Bob were walking faster than David and me. We were over a block and a half behind. I know Mabel had said, "I want no more duck's feet, buried eggs, or seaweed."

In her excitement to get there, Mabel fell. Bob began to cry out, "Marj, Marj, Marj!" He was wanting me to come and help. We were far enough back that we didn't hear him; however, the Chinese in the street heard him. Suddenly, dozens of Chinese were running in our direction, hollering, "Marj! Marj! Marj!" David said, "It sounds like they are saying Marj, but they can't know your name. Do you think it is a Chinese word? I wonder what it means." "Marj! Marj! Marj!" they continued. And we finally realized they were all running right toward us. It finally dawned on us that something must be wrong up ahead. Then, we began to hurry and got there to find Mabel splat on the sidewalk. Bob was not letting her move. I asked, "Mabel, do you think anything's broken?" "No," she answered. "Make him let me get up. In fact, help me get up. Let's go get a steak."

We helped her up, and she appeared to be in fine shape, just bruised and embarrassed.

We had a wonderful dinner, and we had a real good laugh over thinking "Marj" was a Chinese word.

The Piano and I

My mother always wanted to teach piano lessons. She played a little bit and enjoyed it. I can remember her playing "There's an Old Spinning Wheel in the Parlor" over and over. During the Depression years, she thought if she had just learned more piano, she could have picked up a little bit of extra money by teaching lessons.

There was no question in her mind. Marjorie was to take piano. So I did. I took piano lessons from Mrs. Stotler, a wonderful teacher who emphasized sight reading, posture, discipline and practice. Ugh.

I had to practice an hour each day. I cheated. I always started practice in the morning right after breakfast at the time that my mother was taking Dad to work to open their Auto Supply Store. So, I had twenty minutes while she wasn't there that I didn't practice, but always said that I did. When I would hear the brakes squeal on our old car as she turned onto Indiana Avenue, I knew she was returning. At the time she left, I was practicing. When she returned, I was practicing diligently. My brother threatened to tell, but he never did. I told him that if he told on me, I was going to insist to Mother that he had to take piano, as well.

My mother managed the finances of the family and did it well. She said I could go to college, if I majored in music. That wasn't my idea. I was already interested in writing and journalism. But I majored in music. I majored in piano and minored in public school music. I took courses in harmony, music appreciation, counterpoint, orchestration, conducting, reeds, string, brass, percussion, and dear knows what else.

At Texas A & I, I had to practice two hours a day. What a low blow. They shut you up in little rooms. In one of the college yearbooks, there is a picture of my friend, Myra Waddell, and I looking out the window of one of those little practice rooms, talking to a couple of guys. But mostly, you practiced. They checked on you and wrote it down on little record pads.

At one point, they told me I had a big honor, and I was to get to take a lesson from a visiting concert pianist who was more or less famous. His name was Peter Somebody. I don't remember his last name, but I'm sure he doesn't remember mine either. He told me that I used the pedal far too much and that they ought to cut off my foot. I didn't think too much of that, but it did make me use the pedal less. I gave a senior recital right before graduation. I played works from Beethoven, Bach, Mozart, Rachmaninoff, Chopin, Bartok, and a couple more. All of it was done from memory, of course, with no sheet music.

My husband-to-be came to the recital with my roommate, and she kept him from clapping when I stopped in between movements in the Mozart Sonata, explaining that you didn't do that.

My parents came. Mrs. Stotler came. They sent flowers. They were very proud.

My friend, Marian Thomas, and her parents gave me a big reception. It was all very wonderful, and I'm glad I don't ever have to do that again.

They had told me to skip classes that day and relax. I relaxed a little too much. I went with my boyfriend and his roommate to the beach and on the way back, the car had a flat. I thought I was going to miss my senior recital.

My roommate, Pat Weikel, had ironed my formal. She had hosted my parents. Everybody was frantic. I came running in, hastily introduced my parents to the two guys. Mother got confused over which one was my fellow. She thought it was the short one and couldn't understand it because I always liked tall men. Well, it was the tall one. She later got that straightened out, but she said the short one was friendlier to her that day.

I got some use out of my music education. I played the piano and did choir work at churches as a volunteer. I actually taught high school choir and public school music in the junior high in Kingsville, Texas, for one year while my husband got out of college the year after World War II ended. My high school choir won a first division in concert. And I still enjoy playing the piano on occasion. So, I did use my music education, but my heart was always in journalism.

In turn, I made all of my kids take piano. After all, I had a piano. My grandmother had left money to buy me a piano whenever I got a home. I still enjoy plunking tunes out on it.

My friend, Margie Duke, is still peeved because my son, Jim Bob, and his friend, Clay Slack, told Craig Duke that "we get to take piano, and it's a lot of fun." They were lying through their teeth. Craig went home and had a fit so they bought him a piano. The last I heard, they still have it. Nobody plays it. They soon found out that neither Jim Bob, Clay, nor Craig, really liked piano.

Ever since I got run over by a pickup driven by a union member after I covered a union meeting and broke my left wrist, I can no longer play Rachmaninoff and some of the more difficult pieces. But I can still play popular music, Texas songs, and hymns, and I enjoy it.

I used to have a party in both Atlanta and Louisville on San Jacinto Day. The invitation read, "If you don't know when San Jacinto Day is, you're not invited." We had a lot of fun at that party, and I always played the piano, and we sang the Texas songs.

My girls fought practice as hard as I had done. My son was worse. He would send word to the piano teacher that he was at the dentist and go play in the park and not go to his lessons. I didn't find that out until the teacher asked, "How come Jim Bob has so many bad teeth?"

But the piano and I go way back. It's always been part of my life. I still like to thump out Christmas songs on Christmas Eve. When I look at my piano in my apartment today, I laugh and sit down and play a tune and say to myself, "Thanks, Mom."

The Computer and I

I resisted for the longest time ever learning anything about the computer, and I still haven't learned much.

When I was still working at the Big Spring Herald out in West Texas in the late seventies, I was frightened when I heard that the newspapers around were all going to computers.

I had a perfectly good typewriter, and I had always been a good typist since high school. And that was the way I wrote. It was rewarding to me to be able to jerk a sheet of paper out of the typewriter, wad it up, and throw it away.

One of the reporters in a nearby town told me that they were now on word processors and that sometimes if you pushed the wrong key, it ate your whole story, and you had to start over. Now, that scared me even more.

Right after I left the newspaper to go to Atlanta and work for the church, the newspaper changed over. I missed it. Thank goodness.

And when I got to Atlanta, happily they were still on typewriters. How I loved it as I typed away news releases and stories for This Week and articles for The Presbyterian Survey.

But trouble began to set in. The church was getting progressive. Computers were sneaking into the building. The really forward-looking Presbyterians were talking about something called PresbyNet. Well, at that time, PresbyNet didn't do anything to endear itself to me. When I was nominated to become news director for the newly-merged denominations, some of my opponents and so-called friends began to say ugly things about me on the PresbyNet network. Vic Jameson, my longtime, good friend and wonderful Presbyterian journalist who was then editing The Survey, came in and showed the messages to me. I said, "Vic, get Bill Gee to put a message on PresbyNet for me. They misspelled Marj. Tell them if they are going to talk ugly about me, to at least spell my name correctly." He put that message out, and it suddenly got strangely silent out there.

I finally was forced to get a traveling computer and a big old printer in the office and began to struggle with learning the thing. I didn't really do too well, but I tried.

When I got to Louisville to the new headquarters, I found that there were going to be a lot of computers everywhere. Fortunately, I had hired David Dempsey, and he was a computer whiz. He would take my misspelled and hurriedly-typed offerings and put them into the computer. It made me look good. But as to computers, I was really stupid.

The last and final year that I worked for the church, they moved me to Mission Interpretation, which I had been doing a lot of anyway. So, I had to learn to use the computer. I worked hard at it. I made a lot of mistakes. I was constantly pushing the wrong thing and having all kinds of disasters. Vann Dyche tried to help me. Merrill Cook, who is also a computer whiz, tried to help me. I felt sorry for both of them.

After that year when I realized I was retiring and moving back to West Texas, I knew I had to have a computer. So, I bought one. I got Merrill to help me pick it out and set it up where I could continue to send Mission News back to Louisville and merge it into PresbyNet.

Still—on occasion—I push the wrong thing and have all kinds of havoc. One day I knocked a wire loose and thought I never would be able to print anything again.

After that, I got a message in my personal notes from an old friend, and it took me three days and some help from Cook to get a message back to him.

Let's face it. I'm a computer illiterate. My grandsons, Chad and Cody, can work one better that I can. But I know computers are here to stay, and I'm using one. I'm using one. I'm using one. Darn it.

The Airplane and I

When you've traveled in 126 countries and all 50 states, you can tell a lot of airport and airplane tales. So I won't tell them all.

I remember when I was a child, we went to the airport in Brownsville, Texas, which is now a very minor airport. At that time, it was an important Pan American Airport in those early days of commercial flying.

Our family friend Pres Allen and I went up in a plane, and I was so excited. I didn't fly again until I was living in Pecos, Texas, and trying to figure out a way to get to South Texas with my children. I flew on what was then called Trans Texas Airlines, which we lovingly called the Treetop Airlines in that state. It was because they went up and down in so many small towns. They flew right into Pecos, which nobody does today.

I had my two little girls with me, and one of them threw up all over me. When people tell me that motion sickness is all in your head, I recall, "But my baby daughter got sick from motion on an airplane, and she didn't even know where she way. It is in your stomach."

Cathy, the oldest child, loved to travel. That may be why she went over and lived in England 21 years and traveled around Europe and the Middle East. When she was just walking, she trotted over and began to beat on the large glass windows at the Harlingen Airport delightedly screaming, "Pairplanes! Pairplanes!"

Well, I've about had enough of those "pairplanes". I guess the scariest time for me was in Ecuador when we landed in a dense fog. It was frightening, and I knew we were going down too fast. We hit the ground so hard that the light fixtures fell out of the top of the plane and the ashtrays bounced out of the arms of the seats. They announced, "We will disembark and stop in this airport until the fog has lifted." I remember thinking, "Thank God."

I wasn't always that happy over delays. And I would fight to catch plane connections. I remember one time in a smaller city in Colorado, they announced that my plane was not going to Denver. A rival airline ticket counter was next door. I rushed over and found that they had a plane going into Denver right then. I went running back and asked for my bag. I was told, "No, we can't do that. We can't locate it." Well, I saw it sitting on the "round and round", right behind the counter. I crawled over the scales, grabbed the bag, and hollered, "Here it is. Thank you very much." And I ran for my plane.

One night in Cincinnati, I was making a close connection between Delta and Comair, trying to get home to Louisville. They took me in a shuttle out to the end of the line of planes and put me on the wrong plane. The attendant pointed out the error and said it was the next plane. I climbed out, and that plane already was revved up. I stood in front of it. They tried to drag me away, and I was having such a fit that they stopped the engine and let me on. I remember the attendant squatting down beside me and rolling off that bit about fastening seat belts, etc. I said, "I know all that." And she said, "Yes, but I have to tell it."

Once I was on a plane that turned around in the air because an engine went out, and we went back. I've flown in circles until nearly all of the fuel was gone and landed in strange places. I've traveled on a plane in Zaire where you climbed up the side on a ladder like climbing a wall into a hayloft. I've flown on planes in Nicaragua with Greek lettering and was told, "These are the planes Greece did not want anymore."

I've spent nights in cheap motels because the plane wasn't going anywhere. I've sat hours on runways with sweat dripping off of me. I've sat more hours in airports and then had to run at the last minute to a different gate. I've walked and walked and walked and walked through airports and caught little trains with baby buggies shoved in my back. I've walked long distances to change gates only to be told to change back. I've been double-booked in seats on planes. Once I was double-booked with a Mark Carpenter, and the computer just showed, "Carpenter, Mar" and there were two of us. That plane was completely full, and luckily I had gotten there first. Poor Mark. He said, "Lady, I'm going on business, and I'm sure you are just vacationing." Wrong. I didn't move.

I've lost control and shouted at desk clerks and had them shout back. I've also had a lot of help from some really fine personnel who care. They all don't care, but some of them do. Thank goodness.

I've sat eleven hours in an airport in West Texas, trying to make a connection to Merced, California, and I haven't gotten there yet. I've been put on planes and then told to get off because the plane had too much weight. I've been on small planes with just the pilot and wondered to myself what I thought I was going to do if the pilot had a heart attack.

I've bounced around in windstorms and been through electrical storms, and I must say, flying will increase your prayer life.

Once in Colorado, US Air Express announced that they were going to fly on to the city to which I was going, but they would recommend waiting for the next flight because the winds were going to gust up to 60 miles per hour. They needed to get their plane there so they were going. Everybody got out of line, except me. The attendant came over and asked, "Did you not hear the announcement?" "Yes," I answered, "I heard, and I'm going. I need to get there to make a speech at presbytery." He said, "You must not fly very often, or you'd know better." I didn't even bother to answer about the millions of miles that I have in the air. When I got on that plane, the pilot said, "Lady, sit over the wing, and hang on to the seat in front of you." I did.

I remember one time when I was working for the newspaper in Andrews, Texas, there were some Andrews men killed in a private plane crash in Rockdale, Texas. I was assigned to fly down there with a private pilot and get pictures on the scene. We landed on a dirt landing strip on a private ranch and talked a Mexican national into taking us in a jeep to the mountain where the crash had occurred. I remember we sat on bales of hay. When we got to that mountain, an old rancher drove me up to the top in another jeep. We rode on a goat trail on the edge of the mountain. We were about to slide off, or at least, I thought so. He said, as he adjusted his chewing tobacco to another cheek, "Hain't never going to get me on one of those airplanes." And I answered, "Hain't never going to get me back in this jeep, if we get off this mountain."

When we flew out later that day in a fog, just as night was falling, the pilot used the lining of my jacket to wipe the fog off the windshield. He didn't have a rag. Our rancher friend put his pickup at the end of the dirt runway at the edge of a cliff and turned on the headlights, set the brakes, and got out. That was our lighting system. We taxied toward those headlights and went up, up, and up until we were above the fog.

I still believe flying beat that jeep.

Yes, She Was There

Marj was innocently going on a tour into Russia, Uzbekistad, and other locations in 1986 when Chernobyl blew.

As the group got into Frankfurt, they learned about the disaster in Russia and sat down to determine whether to go on with the trip. We voted yes; the next morning we flew in a nearly-empty airplane flying into Moscow. When we got to the airport, it was crowded with people leaving or attempting to leave. No durn fools were coming in.

Some of our group were frightened. Some of us were just plain mad because they upped the telephone costs for calling back to the States to way over $100, so we didn't call. You could hardly get a call through anyway. I learned later that my son frantically called the husband of our tour leader who was Nancy Miller. He asked Robert, "Where is my mother?" The answer was, "With my wife—God help them both."

We went on with our plans. We were there on May 1 for the big parade, and when we saw all of the big shots sitting out in their special seats out in the open, we knew it was probably safe. Actually, the radiation had all blown over toward Norway, Sweden, and Northern Scotland. So on May 1, the guides took us to a spot where we were to stand to watch the parade. You did not pick your spot. They put us behind three rows of Frenchmen, standing where they could see. All we could see was the tops of guns and flags and balloons. We stood and we stood and we stood for hours, while these went by. Finally, I told the guide, I could stand no longer. She was angry, but she took me around the corner to a travel office and said I was to stay there until she came for me. As we went around the corner, for

146

the first time, I could see the parade, and I began hastily to take pictures. She shouted at me, and I went to the travel room. The people were kind and felt sorry for me and gave me a wonderful poster of Moscow at night, which is framed in my dining room today.

When it was over, I got a good shot of the elderly women cleaning up the debris from the parade and sweeping the streets with their homemade brooms. They did keep Moscow clean. Our cities could take lessons.

But once again, my foot was in the petunias. I was in a place where I wasn't welcome. We had quite a trip and a lot of experiences. But everywhere we went, they seemed to be angry at Americans. A few times, we pretended to be English.

When it got to be the day of Orthodox Easter, we wanted to go to the church, and we did, with no help from our guide. It was the same day as the parade, and we went from 1 A.M. to 5 A.M., standing for the entire service. I never stood so much in one day in my life. But it was an experience I would not take anything for having to take part in it.

When we finally left to go home, angry people in the airport weighed everything we had, even our purses. They downed the weight limit and charged all of us over $100 to get out of there. One young college boy had to borrow money from us. We never saw that money again. One woman screamed and cried, but we finally flew away. When we went into the airport in Atlanta, Nancy's husband, Robert, happily met us with a Geiger counter; we didn't click, thank goodness.

I also went back to China in 2003 with a group of five. We went to all the major cities and rode a terrible train to Harbin, near Siberia. It was supposed to be a Pullman, but it was really only three wooden shelves. I was so glad I had the bottom board and didn't have to climb up high.

In Harbin I was able to present the plaque from the Presbyterian Outreach Foundation in a new church built with funds from a Presbyterian Church in Wichita, Kansas. I thought it would be a little country church, but it held 10,000 and included a steeple and bell. They called it the Hallelujah Church, and it was full.

I got to go back to Cuba and unknowingly, got there the same day as Jimmy Carter. Those kind of things just always seemed to happen to me. I never planned them. It made getting around more difficult because he always seemed to be in the spot we wanted to visit. The same thing happened to me in my third trip into Northern Ireland. Bill Clinton was there. And again, traffic was delayed. Schedules were changed, and I thought, "Here I am with my foot back in the durn petunias."

What Keeps You Going

Through the years, I've heard a lot of remarks and questions about the kind of vitamins I must take and other such comments. "What keeps you going?" they ask. Well, it isn't vitamins; it's prayer.

Another thing that has given me energy is touching base all over the world with children and youth. I have already mentioned that I worked with youth groups in churches in West Texas. In Pecos, I had a real strong youth group. I had them so many years, having first taught them in the nursery.

In Big Spring, I built a youth group from five members up to 72 in a period of four years. It was a very rewarding project. It also was one that I did not want to take on. A boy named Hugh Porter asked me after church one Sunday, "Are you going to teach our Sunday School class?" I answered, "I don't think I have time." And he said, "Nobody wants us." So I said, "Alright, I'll do it. But you better be there every Sunday." And he was.

One time when I was out in the world in Kingston, Jamaica, at a very boring meeting where I was taking notes, I became impatient and walked outside to sit on a bench. I was wondering, "What am I doing here?" Then, some of the children from the church school there came and sat all around me, talking and asking questions. I thought, "This is what I am doing here."

I remember that in 1995 when I had just been elected moderator of the PCUSA, I was at Purdue at a Youth Triennium conference. I was only on stage twelve minutes, and I know when I walked onto that stage, some of the youth wondered, "Who is this old lady?"

I spoke briefly from the heart about Presbyterian heritage and mission. And those 3,000 Presbyterian kids stood up and cheered. It was the most rewarding speech I made the entire year that I was out in the world representing officially the church.

Back in the late 60s in Andrews, Texas, I helped four rather mischievous high school youths (Joe, Bobby, Allen, and another Joe) sponsor a teen-age night club. There was nowhere for the kids in that town to go on weekends. They called that night club The Torch. On Saturday night, they lit a torch outside if they had obtained a band, and there was going to be a dance. The kids in town watched for the torch.

I remember one Saturday night that a very conscientious fundamentalist preacher stood out in the highway in front of the club protesting. I went out to talk to him. He said, "Why don't you work with kids at church?" And I answered, "I do, sir. Every Sunday night in Pecos, Texas, I have a youth group with around 24 kids. It's wonderful. On Saturday night here, I reach the lives of over 100 kids. How many are in your youth group?" He simply walked away.

I mentioned that I'd worked with migrant worker kids when I first got out of college. I have seen needy and starving children all around the world. It breaks my heart, but it also has made me count my blessings and keep trying to help and care about those children in need.

Recently, a Presbyterian youth in Hattiesburg, Mississippi, made a report at a presbytery mission conference. He made a very brief speech. He had been down to the Yucatan to help with a project in Mexico. His speech was the shortest and best all day long. He said simply, "I found out that in the United States, we just have too much stuff." And we do. If you don't think so, just try to move.

Another memory for me is a time when a group of us was riding a jeep through South Africa. John Nelson, husband of Moderator Harriet Nelson, threw a Coke can out on the road. She hollered at him, "John, what do you think you are doing?" He answered, "Did you notice that the kids in the last village were making little cars out of soda cans? I just threw them a new toy."

The rest of us started throwing out our soda cans in that area. But it's the children that keep me trying.

All over the world and all over the church and in all of the towns I have lived in, in covering sports, and in everything I have done, youth and children have kept me going. That's what it is all about.

Writing About the Old West

One of the important elements of my writing career was definitely writing about the Old West. I got to be really interesting to me.

When I was in Pecos, Texas, we found out at The Pecos Independent that Billie Sol Estes was planning to start a daily newspaper to try to run us out of business, and that the editor of that paper was starting to call around hunting old pioneer stories.

Well, I started the next day, which was a couple of months before they could get their paper going, into doing old-timer stories. I wrote 104 of them, and they were put in a book in the Presidential Museum in Odessa by the late John Ben Sheppard.

Someone asked me which were my favorites. They all were. I had one story on Billy the Kid buying ice cream from the Women's Temperance Group outside the bar in Pecos. The bar had the only ice to keep their ice cream cold so they protested the bar while using their ice.

I also liked the story of Barney Riggs, who killed several men and was placed in a prison in Arizona. During a prison break, he helped the guards so they let him out. He came home and was in the bar in Pecos when a relative of his reached toward his rear pocket. Riggs thought he was pulling a gun, so he shot him. He actually was reaching for a handkerchief.

Or there is the story of Clay Allison who was buried in Pecos. He was a gun fighter, and his theme was: "I never killed a man who didn't need killing." He died a very ignoble death. While driving home in a wagon with groceries, a sack of flour slipped. He reached for it and fell under the wheel.

I interviewed one woman in her nineties who remembered the last Indian raid on Fort Davis. I also wrote a story about the Miller-Frazier feud and how Miller shot Sheriff Frazier away from the poker table in Toyah. That story was a little bit too pro-Miller for one of Frazier's survivors. She drove in to the paper from nearby Balmorhea with a pistol in her apron pocket, pulled it out, walked up to my desk, and said, "Don't write about Bud Frazier again." "I won't," I said, and this is the first time I have!

When I got to Big Spring, I wrote a daily column called "Ridin' Fence". It had a lot of stories and features, but every Friday, I wrote about some little country town in the area that had sprung up in the early settler's days. Everybody got where they watched for those stories. When I returned to Big Spring after seventeen years of working for the national church, I began to tell a lot of those stories again on a monthly radio talk show. People in that part of the world love the stories of the Old West.

One couple, Ruby and Cecil Allred, used to take me around to locate the various old schools and post offices, or I never would have found them all. Sometimes I went by myself. I always named the Friday column, "Some Call It Knott", or "Some Call It Klondike", or "Some Call It Punkin Center", etc. Finally, one Friday, I got completely lost and spent hours getting back to the highway. That week I wrote, "Some Call It Lost".

One of my favorites in that series was, "Some Call It Loony". One elderly woman said it really was embarrassing to ride the school bus that said "Loony".

But those stories definitely were among the very favorite things that I have ever written.

With My Back to the Wall

Many times in my career I wished I could simply vanish or become invisible. One of those times was back in 1962 in Pecos, Texas, where I was enjoying a morning cup of coffee in a local drug store. I was sitting way back in the corner with my back to the room.

Suddenly, I realized there was a group nearer the door that were bad-mouthing me for my part in the Estes expose'. Some were really after me, and some were taking up for me. I was very embarrassed. It caused me to never again sit with my back to the door. To this day, when I enter an eating establishment or any other room, I always sit with my back to the wall.

Those days were so frustrating. I got into my car one day, and there was a cardboard sign with a green crayola printing on it that said, "This could have been a rattlesnake." I, who am fearfully afraid of snakes, wondered, "What could have been a rattlesnake?" Then I saw an empty box on the adjoining seat, and I saw a grey snake crawling out from under the seat. I went for a hoe and pushed the snake into the box and closed it. I hastily drove to the yard of the gentleman whom I thought had sent me this loving gift and threw the box, snake and all, into his front yard.

On the following morning, which was Sunday, I went to the Presbyterian Church to teach the nursery Sunday School class. A three-year old, whose father worked for the person whom I thought had sent me the snake, came up to me and said, "All snakes don't hurt you."

I knew immediately that the child had overheard the process of sending me a snake and had been told that it was all right. I simply said,

"That's right. All snakes don't hurt you." About ten years later, my son was graduating from high school and went back to Pecos from Andrews to a party being held for some of the senior boys, including him. One of the hosts was the man who had probably left me the snake. We had never said a word. When that gentleman asked my son, "Jim Bob, what are you doing nowadays?", Jim Bob answered, "Well, I'm not putting snakes in cars." The gentleman paled and left the party, although he was one of the hosts.

During that time, one of my daughters spent the night with one of her close friends, whose father was very involved with the Estes camp. When I went to pick her up, I was chatting briefly to the child's mother when she suddenly shoved me into the laundry room and said, "Stay there, please." It dawned on me that her husband had just come home, and she didn't want him to see me in their house. It was really a mixed-up town in those days. She finally let me out of the laundry room, and my daughter and I returned home.

I remember another time I wished I was invisible, and this one was funny. I had been to the San Genarro festival in Little Italy in New York City with my friend, Claire Gartrell Davis, and a Rev. Bill Huie. We were a strange-looking trio. Claire and I are neither one small women, and Bill was a curly-headed blonde with big, blue eyes who kind of strutted when he walked.

We went into a coffee house late that night to get dessert and had to wait to be seated. I remember we were impressed because Gloria Vanderbilt was there and many others. The maitre-d' couldn't seem to get Bill's name straight, and he finally said, "Huie . . . like Huey, Dewey, and Louie." Well, that did it. When they called his name, they said, "Huey, Dewey, and Louie", and we stood to take our table. It brought down the house, and I really wished I was invisible.

Then, I remember being told something one time that I could not share for years. Grant Salisbury at US News and World Report told me in 1964 that at one time a few of them were interviewing Kennedy and LBJ at their editorial offices, and the two got into a violent disagreement. Kennedy is reported to have pointed his finger at LBJ and said, "You will not run with me again." Then, they realized there were a couple of editors in the room and apologized for the whole thing, saying it was just momentary anger. It makes you stop and think . . .

There are so many times that I recall that I either had my foot in the petunias or my back to the wall.

So Slow Down, Marj—Who Sez?

For ten or twelve years or more I preached at some Presbyterian Church almost every weekend and at presbyteries and other meetings in between, pushing "Mission, Mission, Mission". I've spoken at over 6,000 churches, and I'm still getting out there.

A lot of people told me to slow down. Usually, they made this comment, "Marj, I'm so thankful you came. We needed to hear this, but Marj, you need to slow down now." And I'd answer, "Would you have cared if I cancelled coming here?" They would look startled and sheepish and say, "I see what you are saying." I would explain it was very difficult for me to say no to any church or group wanting to hear about mission. So, I kept pushing.

When I fell down the escalator in the Louisville airport and ended up in the emergency room, I slowed down for about ten days. After all, I had bruised my right knee, broken my nose, and broken my dentures. But I got right back up to go to Princeton Seminary where President Thomas Gillespie helped me get to chapel, with me using my walker. Then, I was off again and running.

When I got to General Assembly in Albuquerque and was late to a meeting, I ran out onto a rain-slick sidewalk, fell, hit my right knee again, and hit my face on the curb. I used makeup for the first time in my life so I wouldn't be all beaten up looking to lead the worship service for thousands that Sunday. And it was fine. So, I was off and running again.

I realize now that the constant falls on the right leg had probably hairline-cracked my thigh bone because I began to limp and have a balance problem. But, I kept going.

However, after traveling in 126 countries, uphill and down dale and through creeks and over mountains, and in many difficult circumstances, on October 29, 1998, I fell on the nice, soft carpet in my living room and shattered my femur. Then later, I fell in my own parking lot and got my hip.

Never have I been so frustrated. I began to cancel speaking engagements—first in November—then January—then February and finally, unbelievably, in March. In April, I managed to start back. I'd fallen before but always with just a few hours or a few days of recovery. This was a shocker.

When I got into the third month, still unable to put weight on my right foot, they discovered some of my bones were so soft that the plate was shifting, and my leg was growing crooked. I wasn't ever going to walk again that way. So, I was sent back to another hospital for more surgery. That really was a despondent time for me. "Why?" I kept asking myself. "Why, why, why?" I had to cancel some more talks, and I kept telling myself that there has to be a reason, but I never did figure out what it was. I just began to battle my way back—with wheelchair and walker and cane and guts. One thing that kept me going was over 2000 messages from all over the church. I was overwhelmed. I couldn't believe it, but I was grateful. The local florist had a booming business, and the post office and telephone companies did fine.

Almost all of the messages said the same thing. "Get well. Come back. Come back. We need you."

Well, I thought, at least they have quit telling me to rest. So, I can now go back. You don't quit going because you get old; you get old because you quit going.

And I have rested until my posterior is numb. Then, at the end of 2000, went through it all again with my hip.

But I guarantee you that as long as I can, I'll be off and running. I'll be out there—pushing mission.

The Best Days of my Life

Since I have told stories about a lot of the bad days of my life, I really think I would like to point out the best. It is not a block of time but rather individual best days.

The three best days of my life were the days my three babies were born and were healthy. I lived in Odem, Texas, when Catherine was born. I had to go seven miles to Sinton to the hospital since there was not one in Odem.

The morning after she was born, a hurricane was threatening to hit the Corpus Christi area, which included Odem. She was the only infant in the nursery so they came down and told me that if it hit, they would bring her to my room which had no windows because the nursery was surrounded with glass. My mother was there sitting with me, and we agreed on that, but thankfully, that hurricane veered off and went out into the Gulf.

The second child born was Carolyn, and she was born in a clinic in Pecos, Texas. My doctor and the doctors who owned the private hospital in town were more or less at war with each other. Doctors seemed to do that a lot in Pecos. So, Carolyn was placed in a basket right by my bed. I liked that, and so did she.

The third and last child for me was Jim Bob, born in a brand new hospital in Pecos. It was pre-Christmas season, and I had been working for several Saturdays with all of the Girl Scouts of the city, practicing Christmas carols which they were to sing as the community Christmas tree was lighted. Jim Bob was born that morning so I didn't make the ceremonies. The girls did, however, and afterwards, other Girl Scout leaders brought all of them to the hospital. They tromped across the brand new lawn and sang Christmas carols by my window. I wept as they sang "Away in the Manger". I told my son later, you are the only baby I know that had 100 girls come and sing songs because you were born.

I cherished their successes, like Catherine's being named band sweetheart and Carolyn becoming the drum major she had wanted to be, and Jim Bob being on a basketball team that went to state. A wonderful day for me was when I realized I had paid off all the debts for their college education.

Some of my awards days were special, and some became just routine, as I eventually won over 130 journalism awards. But the first one was special. It was a first for my news coverage of the aftermath of Estes, and I rode a bus all the way to Fort Worth to receive that award. The Associated Press Community Service award was special, as was the very first Associated Press managing Editor's award I won in Big Spring. It was for a short feature about a Native American.

When I won first place in the entire nation in the National Press Women awards for a story about the refinery fire in Big Spring, I was elated. Second and third that year were from Santa Fe and Denver papers, and I went to Biloxi, Mississippi, to receive that award. I didn't have enough money to stay at the convention hotel, so I stayed at a cheaper motel down the beach and hiked up my formal gown and ran down the beach to the award banquet.

I also cherished my first place in Big Spring from West Texas Press for my column "Riding Fence". This was because I enjoyed writing that column more than anything else.

The rest all kind of run together. A "best day" for me was when the church selected me to continue as news director as I left Atlanta and moved to Louisville. At that time there was a lot of competition between the two former offices in obtaining the new slots. That was more important to me than the day I went to work for the church in the first place because by then, I had decided it was what I liked to do. The day I was ordained an elder was also special.

Another special day for me was when a Mexican lad named Andres brought me the ugliest painted seashell I have ever seen. I had rushed him to the hospital when he was injured in a baseball game, and I had paid the doctor. The seashell was special.

There were so many special days as I traveled around the world to over 583 mission stations in 126 countries. I cherish all of them although some I would never want to relive. But I hold close many memories that can bring laughter to my heart or tears to my soul.

The day I was named Woman of the Year by the National Press Women in a meeting in Cleveland was very special. Bess Myerson was speaker at that banquet, and we sat and talked afterwards for two hours.

The day I was elected Moderator of the General Assembly of the Presbyterian Church, USA, was so special to me that I can cry thinking about it. I appreciated the nomination by Bill Henning who had talked me into going to work for the church in the first place. I still feel very, very humble about that honor, and I really worked hard at being an adequate moderator while I presided and the years following while I traveled.

One of the most special of all was in Albuquerque, New Mexico, at the worship service which I led as I finished my Moderator year. The most special moment was when Chad and Cody, my grandsons, helped lead that crowd of thousands of Presbyterians in singing, "Jesus Loves Me, This I Know". If my granddaughter, Dusty, had still been awake in that service, she would have sung it, too, because she knew it.

And you know what? Any day is special if you realize, "Jesus Loves Me, This I Know".

And the Very Best

The very best stories from my life still have to be the wonderful experiences that I was allowed to have visiting the mission fields. My greatest admiration is for the mission workers of the Presbyterian Church, USA, as they struggle, labor, pray, and work with great faithfulness in the world, taking the Gospel to all nations.

This book of stories from my life is dedicated to them and for all they mean to me. Whatever else I have done in this world, I have most appreciated being allowed to tell their stories.

LaVergne, TN USA
29 October 2010
202734LV00004B/88/P